THE CORONATION BOOK

The Dramatic Story in History & Legend

❖❖❖❖❖❖❖❖❖❖❖❖❖❖❖❖

Illustrated with photographs

THE
CORONATION
BOOK

*The Dramatic Story
in History & Legend*

❖❖❖

BY LEONARD WIBBERLEY

Ariel Books · New York

3399

Except where otherwise indicated the photographs for this book have been supplied by the British Information Service, which we gratefully acknowledge.

ARIEL BOOKS
IS A DIVISION OF

FARRAR, STRAUS & YOUNG

Manufactured in the United States of America

*Published simultaneously in Canada
By George J. McLeod, Ltd., Toronto*

Contents

List of Illustrations

Foreword

IT IS difficult in writing a book of this nature to define what is history and what is legend. History we think of as something which is written down and "proven." Yet if those who took part in a particular event centuries or even decades ago were able to speak now, their testimony might well revise much which is written in our history books and accepted as beyond dispute. Indeed, even without such testimony, we are constantly revising history as a result of new evidence turning up.

Legend might be regarded as that part of the story of man which has been passed on from generation to generation mostly by word of mouth and for which no proof has yet been found. Yet the essence of a legend is not necessarily to be discredited because no proof has been found for it.

How could St. George have killed a dragon as related in the legend when there were no dragons anywhere in the world at any time? It is true there were no dragons. But the pythons and other big snakes of the tropics were once found in Europe. Isn't it possible he killed one of them? And was there ever a Minotaur—a creature half bull and half man—in the labyrinth of Crete? No one has ever found the remains of such a monster. But traces of a labyrinth in Crete have been uncovered, and monsters are not unknown according to the Encyclopaedia Britannica.

There are many legends in the following pages, and I have done my best to identify them as such. They have to be there because much of the British Coronation Ceremony and its background outstrips the written and proven record of history. I do not ask that these legends be believed. But on the other hand it would be poor judgment to leave them out, for they are a part of the pageant. For the account of the cursing of William the Conqueror by the Thane of Wulfstan I have been able to find only one authority. The details are related in W. J. Passingham's excellent work *A History of the Coronation* (Sampson, Low. London). On the other hand, the account of the riot outside Westminster Abbey during the Conqueror's crowning is attested to by a number of historians.

In assembling the material for this book, I have consulted a score or more authors, including a great number of newspaper files. A list of the more important books which aided in research is given in a short bibliography at the end. I had some difficulty in establishing facts, for authorities do not always agree. But I have done what I could to get the truth or as near the truth as possible. Despite these precautions errors may have crept in, and if they have, I shall be glad of correction.

Finally my thanks must go to Frank Mitchell of the British Information Services in Los Angeles for much valuable assistance.

Leonard Wibberley

HERMOSA BEACH,
CALIFORNIA.
NOVEMBER, 1952

PART I

*The history and meaning
of Coronations &
the story of the Stone of Scone*

❖❖❖❖❖❖❖❖❖❖❖❖❖❖❖❖❖❖❖❖❖❖❖❖❖❖❖❖❖❖❖

CHAPTER I

The Lord's Anointed

WHEN A BRITISH king or queen is crowned, the past is brought to life again and made to serve the present. Words, originally uttered so many centuries ago that nobody can say precisely when they were first spoken, are repeated for modern ears to hear. Rituals are performed, some of which had their beginnings in the days of the Old Testament. Offices and ranks, formerly important in the government of the kingdom, are revived for the occasion, although now they are largely without significance.

The British Coronation Ceremony is one of the few if not the only one surviving in the world today. It goes back to the earliest European coronations, which, as far as is known, were carried out by the Celtic tribes inhabiting the greater part of that continent before the Roman conquest. These were not really coronations, for no crown was used. Instead they were enthronements or the seating of the new ruler in the chair of authority.

When the tribal chief died, the elder warriors quickly picked a successor. This might be his son, or nephew, or someone not related to him, but who had shown sagacity in council and daring in war. He was seated upon a shield, lifted high above the heads of the warriors and carried aloft in the midst of the people so that they would know their new leader. Sometimes this was done only once, but quite frequently it was done three times, therefore leaving no doubt of his identity. A spear was put into the new chief's hand as a symbol of his authority. Today a sceptre replaces the spear though the symbolism remains the same.

The people hailed their new leader and swore that they would serve him and fight for him. And so that all would know him, the chief grew his hair longer than the other warriors and dressed it in a different way. Sometimes he wore a diadem, a richly worked cloth, around his forehead. The diadem might be called an early kind of crown.

The shield on which the ruler sat was the earliest coronation chair or throne. Now it has been replaced by a real chair. But when a British monarch is seated on the Coronation throne before his or her people in Westminster Abbey, the act has the same meaning as when the ancient Celtic chiefs were carried on a shield over the heads of their subjects.

Christianity brought to the old coronation rite a new significance, transforming what used to be a purely civil and military ritual into a religious service. He or she whom the people chose as their ruler was consecrated to the Ruler of all peoples, anointed of the Lord.

Today, the ritual of crowning and seating the monarch on the Coronation Chair, once the essence of the ceremony, no longer actually makes a sovereign. Queen Elizabeth II became the Queen of Great Britain by proclamation immediately on the death of her father, George VI, on February 6, 1952. Two English kings were never crowned: Edward V, who ruled in 1483, and Edward VIII, who abdicated before his coronation and is now the Duke of Windsor. A far more important part of the ritual is the anointing, which is done with oil by the Archbishop of Canterbury. This sets the monarch apart from all others as one to be revered and served.

The anointing of the king or queen at the coronation is traced directly to the anointing of David and other Jewish leaders in the Old Testament. It is hard to say who was the first of the English kings to be anointed. Possibly it was Aethelbert, the pagan king of Kent, who in 597 A.D. received St. Augustine, a missionary from Rome, and was converted to Christianity. For nearly fourteen centuries, however, the kings and queens of England have been dedicated in this way to God.

Around the anointing, in which a special oil is used, a strange story has sprung up.

It is related that one night in the twelfth century, the Virgin Mary appeared to Thomas à Becket, who was Archbishop of Canterbury, and gave him a vessel containing holy oil, telling him that it was to be used for the anointing of kings. The Archbishop reported his vision to the Pope, and it made such an impression in Rome that years later Pope John XXII set down a full account of the story in a letter written in 1318. This holy oil, if it ever existed, has long since been used up.

The oil used in the anointing ceremony now is called chrism. A mixture of olive oil and balsam, it is blessed by the Archbishop of Canterbury and put aside in a special vessel called the Ampulla.

Because the monarch was anointed with holy oil, and thus consecrated to God, the belief arose that he or she was capable of curing an illness called "the King's Evil." This was the disease known in the old days as scrofula, which is identified today as tuberculosis of the lymphatic glands. Through the centuries, hundreds of people each year would call upon the king to be touched by him and cured of this condition. And the belief in the cure persisted until the first part of the eighteenth century. Dr. Samuel Johnson, who compiled the famous dictionary bearing his name and was a sufferer from this form of tuberculosis, was touched by Queen Anne in the hope that he would be cured. But no cure was effected.

The French also have a legend concerning the anointing of their kings, although France is now a republic and has no monarch. According to the story, the pagan Frankish King Clovis, who lived from 466 to 511 A.D., took an oath that he would be converted to Christianity if he were victorious in a critical battle over his enemies. After the battle, in which he achieved a decisive victory, Clovis went to the city of Reims where he was baptized on Christmas Day, 496, together with three thousand of his warriors.

It is related that on Christmas Eve a dove flew into the Cathedral of Reims carrying in its beak a vessel containing oil, which it placed upon the altar. This oil became, the story said, the sacred oil for the anointing of French kings. The fable is a touching one, but it has been established that it was the invention of the Archbishop Hincmar of Reims who lived some three centuries after Clovis died!

In earlier days, the English coronation used to be called the "hallowing" meaning "blessing." The word is the same as occurs in the *Lord's Prayer* ". . . hallowed be Thy name."

The form of the Coronation Ceremony is given in the last chapter of this book. There, it will be seen that the blessing of the monarch is one of the most important parts of the service.

CHAPTER II

The Stone and the Chair

A CROWN is needed to make a king or queen of England, but a block of stone, not much bigger than a suitcase and about the same shape, is necessary to make him sovereign of Scotland. This rock is twenty-six and a half inches long, sixteen and a half inches wide and eleven inches thick. It is rather badly cracked along one side, and so many pieces have been chipped off by souvenir hunters that the edges are quite rough. In color, it is a dark red or purple, and two iron bolts have been driven into each end with a ring inserted in each of them.

This oblong rock is called the "Stone of Destiny" or the "Stone of Scone" (pronounced *skōn*) and, if it could talk, it could tell tales that would stir the world; tales that might revise whole passages of history books; deeds long forgotten and the words of people who lived one thousand years ago. For the Stone of Scone is incredibly old—eleven hundred years by the most cautious reckoning and quite probably older than that by several centuries. Its story covers much of the history of England, Scotland and Ireland and, if legend is to be credited, touches on Biblical history too.

Just where the Stone of Scone came from nobody can say with certainty. The first part of its story should not be taken as fact. It is purely folklore.

According to the legend, the stone first appeared at Bethel in Judea where it was lying on a hillside. On this stone the patriarch Jacob rested his head when he had his dream of the ladder let down from heaven. After his vision, the stone is supposed to have been transported into Egypt by Jacob's countrymen and to have come into the possession of one Gathelus, the son of King Cecrops of Athens, who married Scota, the daughter of Pharaoh.

Gathelus and Scota, alarmed at the growing might of Moses in Egypt, are said to have fled to Spain, taking the holy stone with them. And from there one Simon Brech, a favorite son of Milo, the Scot, carried it from Birgantia in Spain to Ireland. Off the coast of Ireland, so the story goes, Simon Brech's vessel was caught in a storm, and to prevent it being swept up on the rugged Irish coast, the stone was cast overboard as an anchor.

What happened to Simon Brech and his ship is not related, but the legend says that the fury of the tempest was such that the Stone of Scone was torn up from the bed of the sea and thrown on dry land. Here it was found by the ancient Scots who were the original inhabitants of Ireland and who subsequently gave their name to Scotland, a land which they invaded later and settled.

The Scots, impressed by its size and shape, took the stone to the holy hill of Tara on which their kings were crowned and made of it a coronation seat for their kings. There the stone remained for many years until it was once again transported from Tara to Cashel Abbey, how or why is quite uncertain.

At this time, another curious legend arose around the stone. For it was held that whenever a true king sat upon it, the stone would cry out to acknowledge him as a rightful sovereign. But if an impostor sat upon or touched it in any way, the Stone of Scone would remain silent.

How long the stone remained at Cashel Abbey, the legend does not say. But one day there appeared in Ireland, at the head of a host of warriors, a chieftain named Fergus, who pillaged the land. He came from Scotland and seized the stone, carrying it back to his castle at Dunstaffnage.

Now the Stone of Scone emerges from the mist

of legend into the landscape of history. Around 840
A.D. Kenneth I of Scotland, the first of the Scottish
kings, took the stone from Dunstaffnage Castle to
Scone, the capital of his kingdom, and here it received its name, the Stone of Scone. He made it
the official coronation seat of the Scottish kings. No
king could rule in Scotland who was not crowned
over the Stone of Scone and so the stone became the
greatest treasure of the Scottish people.

Then, in 1296, Edward I of England, one of the
most warlike of the feudal monarchs, invaded and
conquered Scotland. Edward was a tall, handsome,
soldierly king who spent almost all his life in war-
fare, fighting sometimes against the French, sometimes the Welsh, sometimes the Scots. Hearing that
the Stone of Scone was held in such high reverence
by the Scots and believing that they could never
have another king if it were removed, Edward ordered the stone taken to Westminster Abbey in London. He had already proclaimed that the King of
England was the overlord of the King of Scotland,
and he hoped that by having English kings crowned
and seated upon the Stone of Scone, they would become the kings of Scotland, too. It did not happen
that way, for the Scots fiercely resisted union with
the English crown for many centuries afterwards.

When Edward returned to London, he ordered a
chair made which would contain the stone. This became the official Coronation Chair. A platform was

built for the stone immediately under the seat, and the man commissioned to make the chair was one Walter the Painter. He was paid five pounds for his work—about fourteen dollars, though the sum was worth much more in those days than now.

The chair and the stone have remained in Westminster Abbey to this day. The chair is the oldest piece of furniture in the Abbey. It has been repaired many times in the past seven centuries, but it is still substantially the same as when Edward I paid his five pounds for it.

For nearly seven hundred years then, the chair has been in the Abbey with the stone beneath, and all but two monarchs crowned on it. In all that time, they have been taken out of the Abbey only twice.

The first time, chair and stone were removed together. That was on December 16, 1653, when, after the English Civil War and the beheading of Charles I, Oliver Cromwell who led the revolution was proclaimed Lord Protector of the Realm under a commonwealth that recognized no king or queen. Rather than have his installation ceremony in Westminster Abbey where the monarchs were traditionally crowned, Cromwell ordered that the Coronation Chair and the Stone of Scone be taken from the Abbey to Westminster Hall, hard by, and that the ceremony be held there. Afterwards, both chair and stone were returned to the Abbey.

The second time, the chair was removed for safe-

keeping during World War II but has remained
there ever since. The stone also was removed but
once more. On the morning of Christmas Day, 1950,
all Britain and, indeed, all the British Empire was
stunned by the news that the ancient Stone of Scone
had disappeared.

One of the greatest searches in the history of Scotland Yard was immediately undertaken to recover it.
Every nook and corner of London and of every city
and town of England, Scotland and Wales were
searched. Rivers were dragged. Guards were placed
at ports and railroad stations. For the first time in
centuries, the borders between England and Scotland were closed, and all who passed over were subject to questioning. Lakes were dredged and one
big lake in Hyde Park, not far from the Abbey,
yielded a stone which looked like the missing Stone
of Scone but turned out to be a piece of masonry.

There were not many clues to go by. A man's stain-
less steel wrist watch was discovered near the Coronation Chair. There were some marks on the floor of
the Abbey where the stone had been dragged, and a
piece of it was found nearby. A man and a woman
had been noticed seated in a car near the Abbey
the night before the theft. That was all.

The days dragged on into weeks and then into
months and still no trace was found of the Stone of
Scone, the national treasure essential to the coronation of British monarchs. The police were much ham-

pered in their detective work by pranksters. A quar-
ryful of imitation Stones of Scone turned up in the
oddest places—one on the steps of the British Mu-
seum. And an American stonemason, Mr. E. B. Ad-
ams of Goldthwaite, Texas, made a replica of the
stone and offered it to the British Ambassador to re-
place the original. But that disappeared, too!

Eventually, after the most careful sifting of evidence, the net started to tighten around the adven-
turers who had taken the stone. Then on the morning of April 11, 1951, three men appeared at the
ancient Abbey of Arbroath in Scotland and, to the
surprise of the custodian, placed a heavy oblong
block upon the high altar. It was the Stone of Scone!

The custodian was so taken aback he forgot to de-
tain the men or even ask their names, but Scotland
Yard already knew them. They were three young
Scotsmen who had taken the stone to focus attention
on the demands of Scottish Nationalists for a greater
measure of self-rule for their country. They had con-
cealed themselves in the Abbey when it had closed
for the night and then taken the stone away, leaving
through a small side door which they had learned
would remain open.

The question next arose as to whether these three,
and the girl who had been with them, should be pros-
ecuted for making off with so precious a relic. The
three young Scotsmen, however, Ian Hamilton, a stu-
dent at Glasgow University, Gavin Vernon of Kin-

loch Rannock, Perthshire, and Alan Stuart of Barrhead, maintained that they had done nothing wrong. They pointed out that the Stone of Scone had belonged to Scotland in the first place, and they added that under the Treaty of Northampton, concluded in 1328, the stone was to have been returned to Scotland but that that provision of the treaty had never been honored. Eventually, it was decided that since the stone had been recovered no further action would be taken—a decision that was heartily cheered in the House of Commons in London.

So the stone is back in its proper place now, under the Coronation Chair, ready for future crownings, and, in a curious way, one of the stories surrounding it has come true—though in reverse. That is the legend that if the stone is sat upon or touched by a rightful sovereign, it will cry out; but if touched by an impostor, it will remain silent. For now, if the stone is touched by an impostor, it cries out, while if touched by a rightful sovereign, it remains silent. The Stone of Scone has been wired for sound and fitted with a burglar alarm!

PART II

The story of the Royal Jewels of Britain

◆◆◆◆◆◆◆◆◆◆◆◆◆◆◆◆◆◆◆◆◆◆◆◆◆◆◆◆◆◆◆◆◆◆◆◆

CHAPTER III

The Black Prince's Ruby

THE RUBY of the Black Prince is as red as blood. It glows in the front of Britain's Imperial State Crown, which all kings or queens wear when they leave Westminster Abbey after their coronation. It is as big as a hen's egg, yet it is not a beautiful thing. No facets have been cut on it, and there are no sparkling points of crimson to be seen. It is like a piece of deep red glass—old, sultry, almost malevolent.

This is the story of the ruby—a tale of heroism and of terror, of good in a strange alliance with evil. It is a true story in all but those details which, with every such account, must be filled in by deduction and imagination.

Edward of Woodstock, Prince of Wales, called the Black Prince because of his sable armor, was seated in the autumn of 1366 A.D. in his private apartment in the monastery of St. Andrew in Bordeaux. With him were such of the knights and commanders in his army as he was accustomed to admit to his confidence. There were Sir John Chandos, a lusty warrior whose deeds were known as far as the borders of Hungary; Sir William Felton, grizzled veteran of a dozen battles; big John de Hastings, whose shoulders were like a bull's; and perhaps half a dozen more.

Through a stained glass window behind the Prince, the sunlight filtered in patterns of gold, blue, red and emerald, lighting a parchment which he held before him. He was a large man with a square, quiet face—a determined face and yet there was a gentleness about it that was almost childlike.

"I am asked," the Black Prince said, "to attack Spain. To be more to the point, to attack and conquer Castile." He spoke calmly, as if this were an invitation to nothing more than a joust for pleasure and the honor of a lady.

The knights looked at each other with surprise—surprise mixed with pleasure. They, with the rest of the English army, had already taken much of France. It was ten years since the Battle of Poitiers and this

The Coronation Chair and the Stone of Scone.

PLATE I

Oliver Cromwell.   *Captain Thomas Blood.*

PLATE II

William and Mary being offered the Coronation Crown by Parliament on February 13, 1689. Engraving from a painting by J. Northcote.

An old engraving of the King's Champion as he performs the Ceremony of the Challenge during the Coronation of King James II.

PLATE III

Queen Elizabeth I wearing state regalia, from an old engraving by Rogers.

PLATE IV

garrison duty on which they were now engaged did not add much lustre to their arms. They welcomed a new campaign, but they knew the Black Prince. He did not make war for war's sake. There must be more reason for it than that. Sir John Chandos put the question, lounging back in his seat and scuffing the rushes on the floor with his feet as he did so.

"In what cause do we take Castile?" he asked. He had no doubts but that the campaign would be successful. The English army, which the Black Prince commanded, had never been defeated. He could not believe that it ever would be.

"In the cause of King Peter of Castile, who has been dethroned by his half brother, Enrique," the Prince replied. "He has written asking our aid. I will read his letter to you."

Coming from a former king to a prince, the letter was couched in strangely servile terms. It was full of lamentation and plays for pity. It spoke of treachery and cruelty, of bribes and deceit. It asked—petitioned would be a better word—the aid of the Black Prince and his warriors in restoring the writer, Peter, to his throne. Although bearing the seal of a monarch, it was the letter of a beggar.

There was silence in the room when the Prince had finished reading. De Hastings rose and walked over to lounge against a wall near the window, rubbing his chin with a gnarled hand. Sir John wiggled a leg clad in chain mail and said nothing.

"Speak boldly," Edward demanded. "Say whatever may be your opinion."

Gradually, reluctantly, the knights spoke up. De Hastings said that Peter of Castile was the same who was known through the whole of Spain as Pedro the Cruel. He had poisoned his wife, killed his brother and sent assassins through every town in his kingdom to murder bishops and archbishops, knights and men-at-arms. It was said of him that when he lifted his foot from the ground, he left a print of blood behind. Sir William Felton stated that no honor was to be gained from espousing the cause of such an evil man, king or no king. The Black Prince, he pointed out, had won for himself the title of the most chivalrous knight in all Christendom. He should not sully his reputation now.

Edward was not convinced. He argued that kings were above other men. They were placed upon their thrones by God Himself and were not to be removed except by death. It would be but attending to the work of the Almighty to return Pedro to his kingdom. Besides, he added, with an Englishman's practicality, if one king is dethroned, who is to say what will happen to others? Who will rise in their defense? Who will pledge homage and service to them?

Seeing their Prince determined on the venture, his counsellors tried to compromise. Let Edward send a message to Pedro the Cruel, now in hiding in Corunna, to come to the English camp and state his case in person, they urged. In that way the Black Prince would be better able to judge the rights and wrongs of the matter.

Edward agreed that there was some justice in this, and a messenger was sent off. But before he could complete his mission, Pedro, himself, arrived at the English camp. He came as a fugitive but, despite the piteous tone of his letter, a somewhat haughty and even magnificent fugitive. He was dressed in a splendid suit of mail, escorted by a company of attendants wearing the royal arms of Castile. And around his neck, on a chain of gold, there hung a ruby—a ruby as big as a hen's egg.

He was fair-haired and fair-skinned, of average height, but with an arrogant ring to his voice. He sat his horse well and talked of dogs and falconry. The Black Prince noticed only two peculiarities about him. When he walked, his knees creaked; when he talked of death, he did so not with pity but warmly and with enjoyment.

The Prince received him with all the attentions due to a king. He was given quarters in the monastery and introduced to the Princess and other ladies of high degree. When these civilities had been attended to and Pedro well feasted, the Black Prince sat late at night with him discussing how he had lost his throne, his present claim to it and the size of the forces which must be overcome before Pedro could return to his kingdom.

There was also the matter of payment. Here Pedro was full of assurances that he would reward the English lavishly for their help if he got his crown back. He would grant to England part of Biscay, especially some seaports on the coast of the bay, and the sum of five hundred thousand golden florins. Unfortunately, he was without possessions at the present time, but later—Pedro the Cruel fingered the big ruby hanging around his neck. He was fond of rubies —rubies and opals—and he had many of them.

In the end, the Treaty of Libourne was drawn up between the two under which the English would try to put Pedro back on his throne. To finance the expedition, the Black Prince, with a chivalry characteristic of him, melted down his own gold plate. But he also undertook, influenced by the warnings of his knights, to give Pedro a few lessons in being a king. "Treat your subjects well when you return to Castile," he said. "Seek their affection by justice and mercy. Otherwise you may lose your crown again."

With the treaty signed, the work of the armorers began. Ten years without a battle had left the English army little but an occupation force. Swords had to be forged, coats of mail made, arrows and bows produced by the hundred score, spear hafts shaped and tipped with steel heads, horses found and food laid in. Then, in midwinter, the Black Prince marched at the head of his army with Pedro the Cruel on his right-hand side.

They were two months in the passes of the Pyrenees, overwhelmed by snows, raked by icy storms, freezing, hungry, immobilized sometimes for days by huge drifts that smothered men at arms and armored knights as if the very elements themselves were set against the venture. But at last the weather broke, the snows abated, and the forces of the Black Prince streamed down out of the mountain gorges onto the plain of Navaret. The sun shone for the first time in many weeks and suddenly there was a mist of green buds on the trees and the sound of bird song in the air. The Black Prince fell to his knees to thank God for His mercy and to ask His help in the coming battle. Pedro sat his horse and thought this a strange performance, indeed.

At Trevino, where Don Enrique, who had displaced Pedro on the throne of Castile, was holding his court, a messenger arrived from the cautious King Charles V of France. He gave details of the English invasion plans and advised Enrique not to risk a general engagement with the forces of the Black Prince, saying it was well and bloodily established that none could prevail against him. Instead he counselled a war of raiding and attrition, sudden attacks and sudden withdrawals. Bertrand du Guesclin, lieutenant

to Don Enrique who had fought against the Englishman, agreed.

But Don Enrique laughed. Fighting from hedge-
rows, he said, was not becoming either to his honor
or his manhood. He would meet the English and
Pedro the Cruel on an open plain and in full battle.
Du Guesclin, a Breton, shrugged. He had survived
many such foolish judgments on the part of princes
and kings in a long and honorable career. He would,
he assured himself, survive another.

The English army, advancing slowly across the
plain of Navaret, was uncertain of the whereabouts
of the enemy. They expected to meet with them at
any time, yet they needed reliable information. Sir
Thomas Felton, his brother, Sir William, and John
de Hastings asked the Black Prince for permission to
take five hundred men on a scouting expedition and
this was granted. When they had gone only a few
miles, they were suddenly surrounded by six thousand Castilian horsemen. Sir Thomas bade his men
dismount and ranged them along the crest of a hill
nearby. He laughed and promised them good sport
for all and a worthy death. His brother, Sir William,
however, shouting his battle cry, plunged his spurs
into his horse and charged the six thousand Castilians. He impaled one on his spear and then was
hacked to pieces before the eyes of the other Eng-
lishmen.

The engagement was then joined and lasted for

three or four hours. Time and again the Castilian horsemen charged but were unable to take the hill from the five hundred defenders. At last the Marechal d'Audenehame and the Begue de Villaines led an assault of dismounted Castilians against the defenders while men-at-arms attacked them from the rear. The double thrust was successful and all were either taken prisoner or slain. The hill is known to this day as Inglesmendi, or "The Mound of the English."

After midnight of the same night, April 3, 1367, the Castilian main army, under four commanders, Don Enrique, du Guesclin, Don Tello and Don Sancho, formed into battle array and advanced on the forces of the Black Prince. The odds were about two to one, seventy-five thousand under the banner of Castile and forty thousand under that of the Prince. The Castilians were well fed and well armed. The English had not known full bellies for three months. Their bows were warped with the winter snows and their arms dulled.

Dawn found the two forces facing each other, the Spanish with their backs to the River Ebro. The gaudy banners fluttered in a light spring breeze, and the sun flashed on armor and crests and arms. Sir John Chandos rode up to the Prince with a roll of silk in his hands. It was, he said, the swallow-tailed banner of a knight. He asked permission to cut off the swallow tails, raising him to the high rank of knight banneret, privileged to display his own colors in a field of battle.

The Prince passed the banner to Pedro, who with his sword cut off the swallow tails, thereby promoting Sir John, who returned jubilantly to his men crying, "Gentlemen, behold my banner and yours! Guard it as becomes you!"

The armies then moved at walking pace towards each other.

The Black Prince rode with his reins slack across his charger's neck. His hands were folded before him in prayer. When he had finished, he rose in his stirrups, drew his sword and cried, "Banners, advance in the name of God and St. George!"

There was a flourish of trumpets, and with cries of "St. George and England" and "Enrique for Castile" one hundred and fifteen thousand armored men met in full charge.

The Prince, with Pedro screaming his hatred at his side, led his men into the heart of the two divisions commanded by Don Tello and Don Sancho. The Spaniards broke under the fury of the attack. Then the Black Prince swung right to where the division under the command of his brother, John of Gaunt, was being thrust back by the Breton, Bertrand du Guesclin, and his warriors.

The air was filled with English arrows and stones from Castilian slings. Pedro fought with the ferocity of a devil. Enrique tried with equal courage to rally his men, but it was to no avail. The fear of Pedro the Cruel was upon his army, and under the fury of the English attack, they fell back towards the river. There they tried to make a final stand but were pressed so hard that the foremost ranks crowded those in the rear into the swift, chilly waters. Thousands were drowned.

When the battle ended in a complete victory for the Black Prince and the knights withdrew from the field, Pedro the Cruel still ranged over it like a madman. He struck out at wounded and dying men and killed prisoners who came to surrender to him. The sight sickened the English, and they started muttering about fighting for so unworthy an ally and so foul a man.

Bertrand du Guesclin, Don Sancho and others of Enrique's captains surrendered to the Black Prince personally. When Pedro's blood lust had subsided, he returned to the Prince, his armor dripping gore, and sought to embrace him around the knees to thank him for the victory and the return of his throne. But Edward was already seeing the man in a new light. He refused any thanks and told Pedro that the day had been won by the grace of God alone.

Pedro then asked that the prisoners who had surrendered to the Black Prince be turned over to him, as he wished to teach them a lesson. This was refused. Pedro scowled but, overjoyed at the return of his kingdom, took the ruby from around his neck and gave it to Edward as an expression of gratitude. Then he set out for Burgos, an orgy of slaughter and his throne.

Four months later, Pedro still had not paid any part of the five hundred thousand gold florins he had promised the English for their help in retrieving his kingdom. The English army, caught in the heat of a Spanish summer, sickened and many of the soldiers died. The Black Prince contracted a fever. Fearing that his army could not survive another winter's crossing of the Pyrenees, he ordered a withdrawal to Bordeaux. Pedro promised the money as soon as he could lay his hands on it. Meantime, the Black Prince had the ruby.

Back in Bordeaux, Edward's health grew worse. The French revolted, and, hardly able to sit in a saddle, he led his forces against them and defeated them at the Battle of Limoges. But the Spanish expedition, the alliance with Pedro the Cruel, had destroyed him and he knew it. He returned to England, leaving to his brother, John of Gaunt, the management of affairs in France. Seven years later, at the age of forty-six, wasted to mere bones by the fever he had contracted in Spain, the Black Prince died, and all that remained of his campaign was the ruby of Pedro the Cruel.

Recently scientists examined this ruby and made a shattering discovery. They found that the stone, so long cherished, so dearly won, was not a true ruby at all. It was an inferior type of gem known as a spinel.

Pedro the Cruel had proven treacherous to the last.

CHAPTER IV

The Star of Africa

IT HAD BEEN HOT—hot even for the South African midsummer that came surprisingly in January when back in England people were seeking the comfort of coal fires to keep out the breath of winter.

Mine Captain Frederick Wells looked at the wall calendar in his ramshackle field office and noted the date. January 26, 1905. A few months more, he thought, and it would be cool again, and then the work in the diamond diggings at the Premier Mine would not be so stifling and uncomfortable.

Wells had finished the surface inspection that formed part of his duties, and he now had to make the round of the underground diggings. He wished he could put it off, or, better still, he wished he didn't have to make the tour at all. There was really never very much to inspect—he just had to see that the men were out of the galleries and the gear in order and then fill in his report and go home and take a cold bath. The temptation to forget about the underground inspection was especially strong after a hot day like this, but it was a necessary routine. The sooner done, he told himself, the sooner he could get his cold bath. So he picked up a lantern and started off.

He didn't find much: the usual shovel and pickaxe left carelessly on the ground; a new section that looked as though it could do with better propping; nothing out of the ordinary. He started forth again, still carrying his lantern, and then, for the briefest of seconds, in the gloom just beyond the light he saw a flash.

Actually, he wasn't quite sure that he had seen anything. He was tired and hesitated, half persuaded that the flicker of light was just a figment of his imagination. But two years of inspecting in diamond mines had so conditioned him that he could not pass by a flash in a dark tunnel. He turned and raised his lantern. There it was, breast high in the wall, a light with a tinge of fire to it!

Wells took out a pocket knife, put his lantern on the ground and approached the gleam. He half expected to hear a subdued snicker from somewhere in the shaft. The workmen were fond of playing practical jokes—putting a piece of glass in the tunnel wall to reflect the rays of his lantern and make him think he was seeing a diamond. So he wouldn't let himself believe that this was more than a piece of glass. Still, he had to make sure.

Wells cut around the gleaming thing with his penknife blade, and as he worked, his excitement mounted. If this was a diamond, he told himself, it was a monster, almost as big as his clenched fist. Panting now, he worked more hurriedly, digging savagely into the yellowish clay that surrounded the sparkling rock.

Then at last he got the glittering stone out, a stone so big that he could scarcely hold it in his hand, weighing, as near as he could judge, a pound and a half. It was (from what he could see by his lantern) a diamond, the biggest diamond the world had ever known!

He put the huge crystal in his pocket and ran out of the diggings, calling for a boy to drive him to the company's head office. There he found the president of the Premier Mine, Thomas Cullinan, just leaving for his bungalow. Wells pulled him back into his office, shut the door and, to Cullinan's astonishment, commenced tugging at something in his pocket. He had difficulty in getting it out, and when he did, he put on the desk in front of the mine president a monstrous stone that in the light of the room glittered with a hundred points of fire.

The two stared at it in silence—incredulous.

"The biggest in the world," Wells declared at last.

"I can't believe it," Cullinan said. "It's too big for a diamond. Much too big. We'll have to have it tested by every method we know of."

The company's mineralogists were summoned, and that very night the tests were made. The crystal answered to every one of them. There could be no doubt about it. This was indeed a diamond—three times bigger than any ever found before. It was called the Cullinan diamond after the mine president. The experts reported, moreover, that the Cullinan was but part of a much larger stone and that somewhere in the ground there must be another diamond of perhaps equal size—or maybe even larger. That set off a furious search. However, despite every effort, the rest of the diamond was never discovered.

When the technicians turned in their report, Cullinan sent for Wells. "I don't know what your plans are," he said, "but I intend to give you here and now enough money to take care of you for the rest of your life." With that he wrote him a check for forty thousand dollars. Frederick Wells might easily have missed his chance of a fortune if he hadn't stopped to investigate a spark of light in the wall of a tunnel eighteen feet under ground!

Meanwhile, there was the problem of what to do

with the gigantic stone. Diamonds are one of the most valuable of jewels not only because of their beauty but also because of their rarity. The huge Cullinan represented in a single stone more money than any one person was likely to be able to pay for it. Cut into smaller stones, the jewel would lose much of its value. If offered for sale at a reduced price, it would depress the price of diamonds all over the world.

For two years, though the news of the discovery of the monstrous diamond was known in every part of the globe, there was not a buyer to be found for it. Nobody had enough money.

Then General Botha, head of the Transvaal government, who had fought against the British during the Boer War only a few years previously, had an idea. King Edward VII of Britain had just granted to the Transvaal its constitution. In return, Botha proposed that the Transvaal purchase the diamond and make a present of it to the King from the nation with which he had, only a few years previously, been at war.

His proposal was accepted, and the diamond bought. The price has never been divulged, but it is believed to have been around eight hundred thousand dollars.

Next arose the problem of getting the Cullinan to England. The diamond was insured by Lloyd's of London for one million two hundred and fifty thousand dollars. The company's agents had received information that a well-organized and highly efficient gang of jewel thieves was intent upon stealing the gigantic jewel. It could be guarded day and night on its journey to England, but even that might not be sufficient protection. Guards could be killed and bloodshed would not stop the bandits. Some way had to be found of putting the jewel thieves off the scent.

The method hit upon was daring but effective. The diamond was placed in a can which had contained cigarettes, packed in cotton wadding, wrapped and taken as a parcel of no importance to the post office by a minor clerk. He bought a dollar's worth of stamps and sent the parcel containing the diamond by ordinary mail to England.

Then another package, with an ordinary rock inside, was taken under heavy guard to the post office, a form filled out certifying the contents to be of the greatest value, the parcel registered, insured, weighed, sealed, entered in the post office books and an elaborate receipt obtained for it.

The ruse worked. The Cullinan arrived at its destination in London untouched. The worthless parcel was seized by the jewel thieves an hour after being handed over to the postal authorities!

When the diamond arrived in London—addressed to the wife of an official of a bank—it was taken to the bank's strong room to await the royal pleasure. The royal pleasure was that King Edward VII would like to see the stone. Could it please be brought to the palace?

Then came another trip—this time through the streets of London, crowded and snarled with traffic —a perfect opportunity for a smash and grab raid by jewel thieves. So the diamond was insured for two and a half million dollars, and it was delivered to the palace in a man's pocket. All along his route, keeping him always in sight, were plain-clothes men from Scotland Yard.

The Cullinan was brought to the King in his study and placed on a table before him. He picked it up and nearly dropped the heavy jewel. "This is a great curiosity," said His Majesty, "but I would have kicked it aside as a lump of glass if I'd seen it in the road."

Then came the unprecedented task of cutting the huge diamond. Many thousands of others had been cut before, but never one so large and so valuable. It was found that deep in the centre of the stone there was a flaw and the problem was to cut the diamond in such a way as to eliminate this and still obtain as large a gem as possible and a number of smaller stones. The slightest miscalculation on the part of the cutters could readily reduce the value and beauty of the Cullinan by hundreds of thousands of dollars. The House of Asscher in Amsterdam, entrusted with the task, studied the stone for eight months and made a dozen models of it and innumerable drawings before venturing to make a cut.

Although diamonds are the hardest material known to man, they are also quite brittle and can be smashed into a score of fragments with a blow from a hammer. They cleave along certain planes in the same way that a piece of wood will split along the grain. It was to find the precisely right plane along which to cleave the diamond that the Amsterdam cutters spent so long a period of study.

Eventually they were ready and Mr. I. J. Asscher, head of the company, decided to split the stone himself rather than have any of his men burdened with the responsibility. He knew that if anything went wrong, whoever was guilty of the error would be ruined for life. With his son watching, he drew a groove across the top of the Cullinan with another diamond. If the groove were incorrectly placed, the result would be disastrous. Then he took a steel edge, put it in the groove and nodded to his son. The younger Mr. Asscher tapped the steel edge a sharp blow with a mallet, and the diamond fell neatly into two pieces exactly as planned. The flaw in the centre was now in such a position that it would be eliminated in the process of faceting and polishing.

The Cullinan was divided into a total of nine large stones. The biggest of them all, weighing five hundred sixteen and one half carats, or approximately half a pound, was put in the head of the Royal Scep-

tre and given the name of the Star of Africa by
King George V. This is the sceptre of authority
which British monarchs receive at their coronations,
symbolizing their position as the highest in the land.
A smaller stone, which weighed three hundred nine
and three-sixteenths carats was placed in the Imperial State Crown, which is described in a later chapter. Most of the remaining stones were added to
other parts of the Regalia used in the Coronation
spectacle.

CHAPTER V

The Mountain of Light

ONE DIAMOND in the British royal treasure has never been placed in the crown of the sovereign. It is called the Koh-i-nor (also known as Koh-i-noor or Koh-i-nur), which is Persian for "Mountain of Light," and has a strange and terrible story.

Legend says that the Koh-i-nor was found five thousand years ago on the banks of the River Godavari in southern India, but nobody pretends to know who was the finder nor what he did with the jewel. The Mountain of Light, in fact, had no history at all for the first few thousands of years until it leaped suddenly into the ancient records of the East as the most precious jewel of Asia—no common man's gem but a royal jewel, for which kings vied and empires fell and thousands of men died. The jewel brought only reverses and disaster to all its owners, carrying with it a peculiar curse—namely, that whoever possessed it would lose his sight.

In the spring of 1525, Sultan Baber of Kabul in Afghanistan broke out of the Khyber Pass at the head of an army of several thousand men to carve himself an empire on the lush plains of India to the south. At Panipat he met the hosts of the Sultan of the glittering city of Delhi and found himself outnumbered twenty to one. His chieftains proposed that he steal away at night or make a truce with the enemy, returning to Afghanistan with as much of the loot already collected as he could.

Young Baber said he had not come that far merely to run away. He would fight and he would use the new weapons which he had brought with him. The weapons were artillery, never seen in India before, and they served him well. Despite the odds, Baber's guns spread panic among the forces of the Sultan of Delhi, and he achieved so overwhelming a victory that he made himself master of both Delhi and Agra.

With one battle he had won a kingdom. With another he was to win an empire and something more than an empire, a treasure which was to last long after his dynasty and all who knew it had disappeared from the face of the earth.

The Rajahs to the south of Delhi, faced by the

threat of the invader from the Khyber Pass with the new thundering weapons, formed a confederacy. They put aside all their old differences, pooled their armies and marched north to drive Baber back beyond the mountains to Afghanistan whence he had come. The two forces met at Sikri, and once again the artillery of Baber triumphed. Now he was master of an empire which stretched from the Oxus River to Bengal and the Himalayas to Gwalior. All this and one thing else—a huge diamond taken from one Bikeramjit, the Rajah of Gwalior. In Baber's words, the stone was so precious that "a judge of diamonds values it at half the daily expense of the whole world. It is about eight mishkels (186 carats)."

Baber was delighted with the jewel and wore it on his person, a thing as splendid and as barbarous as himself. When he died, he gave it to his son, Humayun. The stone remained the prized possession of the Mogul Empire, which Baber founded, for two hundred years. Its fame and the story of its beauty spread far and wide. But it brought strife rather than peace. In the long line of succession from Baber to the last of the great Moguls, son rebelled against father time and again. The empire was drenched with blood and saturated with cruelty.

Then, in 1739, tempted by the stories of the huge diamond, Nadir Shah, a warrior of Persia, decided that he must own the jewel though he die in the attempt. He swept across Hindustan at the head of a

huge army, captured the imperial city of Delhi in a
few days, sacked it and put the inhabitants to death.
Then he ordered the dethroned Mogul ruler, Mohammed, brought before him and demanded to
know where the famed diamond was. Mohammed
pretended astonishment. The city had been ran-
sacked, he said, the treasure chests rifled, the palaces
plundered. He himself was a captive. How could he
be expected to know now who had the diamond?
The reply made an impression on Nadir Shah, who
was about to leave, content with one hundred and
twenty million dollars in loot which he had already
obtained, when a slave girl whispered to the Persian that the diamond was hidden in the folds of
Mohammed's turban.

It amused Nadir Shah that on top of the head of
the man who now trembled before him was the huge
diamond for which he had searched for days, ran-
sacked a city and destroyed a whole countryside. He
could have readily snatched the turban off Mohammed's head and seized the jewel. But so direct an
action did not appeal to him. He decided that he
would gain the stone by guile; that he would make
Mohammed give it to him of his own free will instead of taking it from him forcibly. That would be a
change of method for Nadir Shah, the conqueror,
and something to set his warriors roaring with laughter when he told them the tale later.

So he completely reversed his tactics. Pretending

to forget about the diamond altogether, he vowed he had no intention whatever of depriving Mohammed of his splendid peacock throne and his fine city of Delhi. Rather, he insisted, he was going to put him back on the throne and proclaim that he was restored to his kingdom.

Mohammed was astonished and refused at first to believe his good fortune, but everything was done as Nadir Shah said. Then a splendid celebration to cement their friendship was held, and, in the view of the assembled courtiers, princes and warriors, Nadir Shah proposed a remarkable exchange. Let Mohammed give him his turban, he said, in return for his own as a symbol of the cordiality and mutual trust that now existed between the two of them.

Mohammed was trapped and had no alternative but to comply with good grace. Reluctantly he took off his turban and handed it to the Persian—and so Mohammed bought his kingdom back with a gem whose value had been estimated at "half the daily expenses of the entire world."

Nadir Shah left the banquet immediately for his own quarters and unwrapped Mohammed's turban. Out of the folds fell the splendid jewel. He held it in the palm of his hand and watched it glitter in the light of a scented oil lamp. "Koh-i-nor," he said, "Mountain of Light." Thus the diamond got the name by which it is known to this day.

The stone brought Nadir Shah no more peace than

it had brought the Mogul emperors. He was one of the greatest of the Persian conquerors, but the loot he obtained from Delhi and the possession of the Mountain of Light acted on him like a poison. From being open-handed and merciful, he became miserly and treacherous. Once, shot at from ambush, his suspicious mind concluded that the trap had been laid by his own son. So he ordered the young warrior to be blinded. He had barely given the order when, in a wave of regret, he tried to countermand it. It was too late, however, and his blinded son came stumbling before him, crying aloud, "My Lord, it is not my eyes but those of Persia which you have put out."

The words proved true. Eight years after he obtained the Mountain of Light, Nadir Shah was assassinated by his own bodyguard, and without his son to take over, his empire crumbled to pieces.

The beautiful but evil stone now passed not to the blinded son of Nadir Shah but to the grandson of the conqueror, Shah Rhuk. He did not have long to enjoy it for the curse of bloodshed and blindness attached to the diamond was now working its full fury. In the fierce conflicts that swirled through the ruined empire of the dead Nadir, Shah Rhuk was himself seized and blinded. He kept his throne, a petty kingdom, but ruled in darkness. He managed to save the Koh-i-nor, for he could not bear to part with the jewel which had given him so much pleasure when he had had his sight, but the Koh-i-nor had not yet finished with him.

A new conqueror arose in Persia—Aga Mohammed, who, lusting for the beautiful diamond, stormed into Khurasan, the kingdom of the blind Shah Rhuk. Shah Rhuk could make no resistance and immediately surrendered his kingdom to the invader. However, it was not the kingdom that Aga Mohammed wanted but the Mountain of Light.

The miserable monarch was fettered in a dungeon and tortured daily until, one by one, he told where all his other gems were hidden. Even though a plaster crown was put on his head and boiling oil poured into it, he refused to reveal the hiding place of the Koh-i-nor. He died as a result of his tortures, but, before he succumbed, he managed to get the diamond to Ahmed Shah, founder of the Afghan Empire, who had remained loyal to the descendants of the great Nadir.

Nevertheless, the curse of the stone was still at work. The diamond came by inheritance to Shah Zaman of Afghanistan, one of twenty-three brothers. Zaman had occupied the throne for only a short time when he was overthrown by one of his brothers, put into prison—and blinded. Before his sight was destroyed, he managed to hide the Koh-i-nor in the plaster walls of his cell, and there it remained while he groped along them, day after day, feeling with his

hands to discover the hiding place of his beloved
jewel. He never found it. A prison guard scratched
his arm on a corner of the diamond one day, pried it
out of the plaster and handed it over to the brother
who had displaced Shah Zaman. No sooner had he
got hold of the diamond than he was himself displaced by another brother and forced to flee for his
life to Lahore—but he took the diamond with him.
There he and his wife were seized by the local Sultan and his wife tortured in his presence until he
parted with the stone. Perhaps to break the curse,
the Sultan paid him the equivalent of forty thousand dollars for the jewel.

The Koh-i-nor remained only a short time in the
treasury of Lahore. The British East India Company,
which maintained its own army in India, after a series of engagements, took possession of the territory
in 1849 and the famous Mountain of Light became
the Company's property. Then arose the problem of
what to do with it. The stone had been the occasion
for war after war, for bloodshed and torture and un-
rest through several centuries. It had brought the
Afghans into India and then the Persians; it had in-
spired the rise of two great empires and then seen
their complete destruction.

A meeting was held in the headquarters of the
Company in Delhi to discuss the disposal of the
Mountain of Light. It was decided to get the Koh-i-
nor out of India so that it could ferment no more

strife and bloodshed, and the directors agreed that the diamond would be presented to Queen Victoria to become part of the royal British treasure. Then somebody asked, "By the way, where is the Koh-i-nor now?"

Sir John Lawrence, to whom the safekeeping of the Mountain of Light had been entrusted when it was taken from Lahore, felt hurriedly through his pockets and his face turned white with anxiety.

"Give me a few minutes, gentlemen," he said. "I have it in a safe place."

He rushed off to his mansion, dashed into the bedroom, startling the Indian valet who was tidying up, and snatched his pajamas off the bed. There, in the breast pocket, wrapped in a piece of paper, was the fateful stone!

The diamond was sent to Queen Victoria under heavy guard. With it went a warning. Shortly before the stone left India, an Indian fakir warned Sir John that if it were worn in the crown of the monarch of England, Britain would lose India.

Queen Victoria took the warning seriously. She left the Koh-i-nor not to Edward, her son and heir to the throne, lest he be tempted to put it in the crown, but to his wife. And Queen Alexandra left it not to her son, who would also become a king, but to his wife, Queen Mary, the Dowager Queen Mother.

At present the gem forms the central setting of Queen Mary's crown. But she has lived to see India split into two nations, Pakistan and the Republic of India, each with a greater measure of independence from British rule than they ever enjoyed before. Now Queen Mary faces the problem of whether or not she should give the fateful jewel to her granddaughter, Queen Elizabeth II. If she does, should she warn Queen Elizabeth never to put the Mountain of Light in the Crown of England? Or has the evil fury of the Koh-i-nor finally spent itself? History may supply the answer.

PART III

How the British Coronation Regalia was once destroyed, then replaced & finally nearly stolen

❖❖

Westminster Abbey.

PLATE V

The Royal Coach shown during the Coronation procession of King George VI.

PLATE VI

The Duke of Norfolk as Earl Marshal.

Captain John Lindley Dymoke, the present Queen's Champion.

PLATE VII

The Coronation of Queen Victoria in 1838 from an old woodcut.

PLATE VIII

Queen Victoria about to receive the sacrament after her Coronation, from the picture by F. Winterhalter.

CHAPTER VI

The Crown Jewels Destroyed

IN ALL the crowd that gathered on and around the scaffold on the afternoon of January 30, 1649, there was only one who had the courage to jest, and he was the King, who was to be beheaded in a matter of minutes.

King Charles I came to his execution in good humor. He had, he maintained, been deprived of his people, deprived of his family, deprived of his throne, deprived of a trial and was now to be deprived of his life. He was amused that this final outrage seemed to worry those who were about to perpetrate it more than it did him who was to be the victim.

From the scaffold outside Whitehall Palace, London, where he stood in the snow, the King could see no one but rebels, as he called the soldiers of Cromwell's Army. Even in his last few minutes, these rebels were going to keep him away from his people. His final words would be heard only by Cromwell's Roundheads who had taken up arms against him.

The King, clad in sombre clothing but with gay ribbons at his knees and fresh lace at his wrists and throat, determined that he would speak what he had to say despite the rebel soldiery. There would be no abandoning of the position which he had maintained through his troubled reign—that kings were appointed to rule by God Himself and that they required no license either from Parliament or from the people for any act which they performed. They could call the Parliament into session or dismiss it, levy taxes or wage war and all because of the Divine Right that belonged alone to kings. That was what he had always believed and he maintained the same position now. Speaking clearly and steadily, he said that he desired the liberty and freedom of the people as much as anyone.

"But I must tell you," he added, "that their liberty and freedom consist in the people having government. It is not in their having a share in the government; that is nothing appertaining unto them. A subject and a sovereign are clean different things."

There were no cheers, no murmurs, nothing but

the sound of the wind in the stiff bare branches of the trees and the uneasy stirring of the soldiers who stood around.

The King gave them a look almost of contempt. He took off his coat to show the rebels that kings also know how to die for what they believe in and put his head upon the block without a tremor. The big axe rose and fell. The snow on the scaffold was suddenly crimson, and the masked executioner stepped forward and picked up the head of the King of England, holding it aloft for the people to see. From now on, England would have no king. There would be a different kind of government under Oliver Cromwell and his army. Nobody knew what kind of a government it would be, but it would not be a monarchy.

There was, the eyewitnesses say, a great groan from the people when they saw the head of the King held up and some of them rushed forward through the ranks of the soldiers to dip their handkerchiefs in the blood of their dead sovereign. The soldiers dispersed them with swords and pikes.

To ensure that there would never be a king in England again, Cromwell decided to destroy the symbols of the monarchy. The Crown, the Sceptres, the Orb, the Ring—all the Regalia used in the Coronation Ceremony would be melted down, and the Coronation robes would either be sold or torn up. However, not everyone who met in the House of Commons shortly after the execution of Charles I to debate the fate of the Regalia was set upon its destruction. Some stated that they would do better to sell the Crown and other pieces intact, as more money could be had for them in that way. The moneylenders of Europe, others argued, were well used to taking royal baubles in pawn.

There was a short discussion and in the end, such was the determination to get rid of all traces of the monarchy in England, the decision was made to melt down everything. The precious metal obtained would be sold in bulk and the jewels individually. Thus, some of the oldest treasures of Europe, dating back almost to the beginnings of English history, were disposed of with little more care than if an attic was being cleared of junk.

Thrown into a crucible and hence lost for all time were the crowns of Edward the Confessor, dating from the eleventh century and of Alfred the Great who ruled from 871 to 900 A.D. Swords, vestments, priceless cups, bracelets and other insignia were disposed of. All that escaped was the Ampulla, or vessel, in which the anointing oil was kept, the Anointing Spoon into which the oil was poured and the Ruby of the Black Prince. The famous ruby was indeed sold but purchased back later. The Ampulla and Spoon were probably just overlooked as having little value. The total obtained for the ancient Regalia of England was around thirteen thousand, two hundred and forty dollars, a small amount even for those days. Then the nation prepared to go ahead and removed all traces of the monarchy.

But the commonwealth which Cromwell established lasted only as long as Cromwell himself. In fact, not quite eleven years after the Crown of England had been thrown into the melting pot, it was decided to restore the monarchy. Charles, the son of the King who had been beheaded and who had been living the life of an exile, was invited to return to the throne. He was proclaimed King on May 8, 1660. However, he could not be crowned until nearly a year later, because there was no crown to put on his head, no robes for him to wear and no sceptre to receive. All had to be made over again, and the task was entrusted to Sir Robert Vyner, who was appointed the royal goldsmith.

It was no easy assignment to undertake because Sir Robert had to find patterns or pictures of all the Regalia which had been destroyed. Then he had to locate diamonds, sapphires, emeralds and jewels of every kind with which to decorate the crown and other pieces. Lastly he had to find the money to finance this work.

The King himself had arrived back in the country with empty pockets. Parliament voted a substantial sum for the work but not without haggling, and Sir Robert was in danger of having to put up some of his own money to fulfill the royal order. As it was, the Regalia was made at a cost of around one hundred and fifty-nine thousand, nine hundred dollars, or more than twelve times the value placed on the royal treasure when it was destroyed by the Cromwellians! It consisted of the essential pieces—the Crown modelled on that of Edward the Confessor, the Orb, Sceptre, swords and other accessories. These, with minor modifications by the succeeding sovereigns, constitute the Regalia of Britain today.

Ten years after Sir Robert had finished his work, the royal insignia were very nearly lost again to one Captain Tom Blood.

CHAPTER VII

Captain Blood

TOM BLOOD was sprawled in a chair in his lodgings not far from Piccadilly, denouncing the fog, the cold, the lack of employment for a professional soldier and the thinness of his purse.

He was a big man and a bold one. Active and fond of adventure, he found life dull in the year 1671 and the prospects of mending his fortunes poor indeed. Twenty-five years before he had commenced his military career as a soldier in the army of Oliver Cromwell, during the Civil War. He'd done well— fought at Marston Moor and Naseby, filled his pockets with the riches of the manors which had fallen to the Cromwellian soldiery and maintained himself in the good graces of his commander by shaving his head and reading frequently and ostentatiously in his Bible.

Later, when the war was over and he had retired with the rank of captain, he'd lived high and handsome from his loot and, it was rumored, sold his sword for the settling of private grievances when the pay was right. But that kind of business had fallen off recently. Probably, he reflected, it was because he'd failed in his attempt to hang the Duke of Ormonde at Tyburn. Blood chuckled when he thought of that venture. If successful, it might have made him the greatest man in England.

Ormonde was Lord Lieutenant of Ireland and Commissioner of the Treasury and the Navy—one of the new nobility who had been created with the restoration of Charles II to the English throne. But Ormonde, by his policies in Ireland, had incurred the royal displeasure, and Blood had been approached with a proposition to kill him in return for a sum of money.

Just whom the proposition came from, he never quite knew and never really tried to find out. What he did know was that the King did not like Ormonde, that the money offered for the deed was handsome and that, if he succeeded, he was likely to stand high in the royal favor.

A simple assassination of the Duke was not suited to Blood's personality, however. He conceived that, instead of running Ormonde through in a duel or perhaps shooting him as he rode in his coach through the streets of London, he would capture him and hang him publicly like a common criminal on the gallows at Tyburn.

He very nearly succeeded. He had personally dragged the Duke from his coach in Piccadilly, tied him to the back of a horse and driven him to Tyburn. In fact, he was even readying the noose when the Duke struggled free, the ducal servants having arrived to rescue their master. Actually, he, Blood, had been lucky to get away with his life.

Of course, there had been no pay for the venture. Furthermore, the captain was in disfavor now because he had failed. Noblemen were avoiding him and his only method of earning a living was to turn highwayman or footpad. He didn't like the prospect of either. A gentleman may be a blackguard, he told himself, but he must in the final analysis remain a gentleman. Skulking in alleys with a loaded pistol under his cloak, waiting for a fat merchant to pass by, went as contrary to his nature as shooting a duke instead of hanging him.

"Parrott," he roared to his companion, "another glass of burgundy, and light the candles. The darkness and gloom of this place weary me."

Parrott, a short, white-faced man with a broken nose, brought a bottle from the sideboard and lit the candles. Blood poured himself some of his favorite wine, the ruddy color of which went so well with his own surname, and watched it splash into the glass.

"Liquid ruby," he said. "I delight in the color of it. Parrott, if I could lay my hands on but one good ruby—a big one, the biggest in the world—believe me, I would be content for the rest of my life. No, don't laugh. I would not sell it but would keep it by me, to warm my heart and give wings to my soul."

"You'd sell it for wine, lace, clothes, horses and perhaps women," said Parrott, a practical man who had fought side by side with Blood in the Civil War and who stayed with him largely because he could think of no good reason for leaving. "In any case," Parrott continued, "there's little likelihood of your finding such a ruby—nor a pearl, nor a diamond, nor an emerald, either."

Blood laughed. "As to that," he countered, "I know of rubies, diamonds and other baubles, lying almost unguarded within a few miles from here. All that is needed is the courage to take them. Two desperate men such as you and I, Parrott, comrades of misfortune, neglected swords, could have them in a twinkling and live royally the rest of our lives— albeit not in England."

Parrott said nothing. He poured a little more of the burgundy into Blood's glass and leaned forward at the table, listening.

"Yes," continued Blood, "jewels fit for a king. In point of fact, the King's jewels."

"The King's jewels!" cried the other.

"Oh well, they call them the King's jewels," said Blood easily, "but they really belong as much to you and me as to King Charles II. They were bought for him a few years back for his coronation and with money obtained from the people through one kind of tax or another. You may see them any day you wish by going down to the Tower and asking. There's an old fellow down there by the name of Talbot Edwards, who takes you round to look at them. And there's a rag-taggle guard that's mostly drunk to protect them. It would not be a difficult task to get them away. Then a quick ship to Europe and after that, a life of luxury—though, mark you, I won't be parted from the rubies. There'd be diamonds enough to keep us in splendor."

The two drank more of the wine and talked more of the project. So, by the time the candles had burned to half their length, the plan to steal the royal jewels of England was complete.

A few days later, Blood, Parrott and a woman who posed as Blood's wife introduced themselves to Talbot Edwards, Deputy Keeper of the Jewel House in the Tower of London, with a request to see the treasures of the Monarch. Edwards, bent and white-haired, always anxious to display the jewels, for it gave him a sense of importance to do so, readily agreed. Hardly had the party started to the Jewel House, however, when Mrs. Blood complained of a sudden attack of nausea. The old jewel keeper gallantly suggested that he take her to his private rooms to rest a little. Meanwhile, he was sure, the gentlemen would not mind waiting until he returned.

Blood and Parrott agreed, expressing gratitude for the kindness offered. As soon as they were alone, they made a quick survey of the Jewel House, noted where the guards were stationed—there were none in the Jewel Room itself—and which was the quickest way to get down to the river. They had completed their survey by the time Edwards returned and showed them the Regalia. They asked a few casual questions about values and whether or not special precautions were not taken to guard the royal gems. To this Edwards replied with a laugh, asking them who would be fool enough to think he could steal the Crown, Sceptre and Orb of the King of England and think he could get away with it. Blood shrugged his shoulders and admitted that the question was foolish.

After this initial inspection, Blood and his party left with many thanks to Edwards for his kindness to the captain's wife. A few days later, Blood returned with a present of a pair of gloves for Mrs. Edwards, and this courtesy led to frequent visits and exchanges of gifts between the Deputy Keeper of the Jewel

House and the captain. They became close acquaint-
ances and, indeed, firm friends.

During one of his visits to Edwards' home, Blood
made some mention of a young nephew, a man with
an income of three hundred pounds a year, safely
invested. It was time, said Blood, that he settled
down and took himself a wife and he could think of
no better match than a marriage between Edwards'
daughter and his nephew.

Edwards took immediately to the idea, for the
three hundred pounds was a big attraction. He was
getting on, he said, and had not put much aside to
look after his daughter. He'd like to see her safely
married before he died. So it was agreed that the
nephew should be brought for introduction to the
young woman and her parents.

On the day set, Blood arrived with Parrott and
two other companions. They were all well mounted
and perhaps a little too well armed for such an innocent occasion. Each carried pistols as well as sword
canes and daggers.

The details were arranged to the smallest scruple.
One of the men, Hunt, pretending to be a servant
of Blood, was to hold the horses. Parrott was to seize
the Orb—a ball of solid gold with a cross atop it.
Blood was to take the Crown. The fourth man, the
prospective bridegroom, had with him a pair of
strong pincers. With these he was to cut the solid
gold Sceptre into pieces and slip them into a bag.

On arrival, Blood said that his wife was delayed since, being in delicate health, she was coming by coach. He proposed that, pending her arrival, they might look once more at the jewels which never failed to impress him with the glory of England. Edwards, ever ready to display his treasures, agreed, and the four set off for the Jewel House.

Blood had already noted that, when showing the treasure to visitors, Edwards always entered the Jewel House with them and locked the door on the inside. He did this now, and, as he was stooping down, working the big key in its stiff lock, Blood struck him to the ground with the butt of his pistol. He fell without as much as a groan. Quickly Blood snatched the glittering Crown and thrust it under his cloak. Parrott grabbed the Orb. The Sceptre, however, was a tougher proposition than had been anticipated. Made of solid gold, it could not readily be cut even with the aid of the pincers brought for the purpose.

While they were struggling with it, Edwards regained consciousness and commenced to call for help. Then the one coincidence for which Blood could not possibly have been prepared occurred to save the royal jewels of England.

Edwards had a son, whom he had not mentioned to Blood, who held an important post in Flanders. The son had chosen this particular day and this particular hour to return unexpectedly to visit his parents. Hearing the uproar in the Jewel House, he called for the guard and dashed in, sword drawn. Blood thrust him aside and plunged out, the Crown under his cloak, followed by his two accomplices. A guard challenged him, and Blood ran him through with his sword cane. But he was hampered in his struggle by the Crown, which fell and went rolling across the ground. Gems rattled out of their settings onto the rough cobblestones. A sweeper later found a diamond worth a fortune, and a trooper picked up several others. Several precious jewels were so trampled into the ground during the scuffle that they were never recovered.

Blood and his accomplices were overwhelmed when reinforcements arrived. Hunt tried to get away on one of the horses but was thrown when his mount reared up in fright at a pistol shot. Parrott was captured with the Orb in his pocket. The attempt to steal the crown jewels was a failure—but only just.

Caught red-handed in the very act of perpetrating such an infamous crime, Blood was locked in the Tower and when the news of the adventure reached King Charles, His Majesty was so intrigued at the daring exploit, that he sent for Blood to interview him, himself. Monarch and thief liked each other immediately. Blood, following his conceptions of a gentleman even in his direst moment, made no attempt to plead for his life.

What went on between the two at this strange interview has never been recorded. Possibly Blood complained about the lack of money and employment for a gentleman adventurer. He may even have reminded the King that when His Majesty was in exile, he also had known the indignities of a thin purse. He may have suggested that the people of England had as much right to the jewels as the King himself since they were bought with money obtained from the people.

In any case, Charles made a remarkable decision. He not only pardoned Blood and his companions for their attempt, but he also ordered that Blood should be paid the handsome sum of five hundred pounds a year for life from the royal purse. In return, he extracted a promise that Blood would not attempt to steal the crown jewels again. They parted on the friendliest terms. Thus the Regalia of England was saved for the coronation of subsequent sovereigns.

PART IV

*The story of the Officers of the Crown,
the Heralds and others, who must attend
a Coronation, & the duties which
they are called upon to perform*

CHAPTER VIII

The Lord High Constable

IT WAS a morning more for sorrow than for celebration—a morning of sadness rather than triumph.

A biting east wind cut through the streets of London, sending the powdered snow scurrying over the frozen ground. The marshes on the banks of the Thames by Westminster were frozen, and inside the Abbey the spluttering torches were unable to dispel the winter cold from the place. The Norman knights and barons surrounding William, called the Conqueror, felt fear mingle with the chill as they watched the ceremony at the altar, crowning him King of England.

Christmas Day, 1066, seemed somehow a poor day for the event. Things had not gone well from the start. There were undertones of rebellion everywhere. The Saxons, only recently defeated at the Battle of Hastings where their King, Harold, had been killed, had turned up in force for the Coronation and they were armed as for war. In front of the Abbey they outnumbered the Norman soldiers, who were there to guard William against his new subjects, and their chiefs were among them—the Thane of Wulfstan of the royal house of Godwine and the Earls of Athelny and Witherstone. There was hatred in their blue eyes as they watched the ceremony.

Ealdred, Archbishop of York, officiating in the place of Stigand of Canterbury, whom William would not trust, droned on interminably, reciting the Coronation Service in Latin. William, tall, broad-shouldered, eyed the Saxon nobles grimly and got what comfort he could from the presence of stout Roger de Mortimer and the other Normans.

The time had come now for the actual anointing and crowning, but first Norman and Saxon had to be asked whether they would accept William as their King. Ealdred put the question to the Saxons and at the same time Geoffrey, Bishop of Coutances, addressed the Normans in their own tongue asking, "Is it your will that William, Duke of Normandy, become King of England?" A roar of assent from both factions shattered the silence in the Abbey and swept into the streets outside. There, the Norman soldiers, misunderstanding the tumult and thinking that the Duke had been killed, turned upon the Saxon warriors. Before they could recover, a dozen had been cut to the ground.

Sheer panic now spread inside and outside the Abbey. Women and children, caught in the battle between Saxon axman and Norman knight, went down until the Abbey steps were so slippery with blood that none could stand on them.

Those inside streamed out to join in the fray. Buildings were set afire, and the ancient war cries that had led the Saxon warriors against Viking and Dane now rang out again. The Thane of Wulfstan, old and bent, formed his men in a wedge, himself at the point of it, and led them into the mailed ranks of the Normans. Back inside the Abbey, William the Conqueror remained almost alone, trembling in the Chair of State with a Saxon Archbishop standing above him, continuing the service. He would not be hurried or interrupted, this Saxon Archbishop. His voice almost drowned out by the clash of arms, the screams of the wounded, the shouted war cries, he continued steadily with the ceremony.

". . . govern thyself well and the Holy Church and the Christian people committed by the Lord to thee," he said, and the Duke half rose from his chair.

"This can wait!" William cried. "I must be out and restore order! We are outnumbered and may lose the day!"

"This ceremony cannot wait," the Archbishop chided. "Unless properly crowned in all the ancient forms, you are not King at all." He continued unhurried, unmoved, through the anointing, the crowning and the benediction. When he had done, William thrust Crown, Sceptre and Orb into the hands of the Archbishop and ran out of the Abbey. There he found that Roger de Mortimer in his absence had taken charge of the Norman forces, but the battle still raged. He leapt on the first horse he found, wielding his sword over his head and crying, "Peace! Peace!" Norman and Saxon, seeing him take the field, broke off the engagement. However, already many were dead and the hatred between the two factions had been intensified, for each accused the other of treachery.

White with rage, William rode over to where the tattered banner of the House of Godwine fluttered in the bitter east wind. A group of Saxons stood huddled around it and gave way to him only grudgingly. At the foot of the banner lay the old Thane of Wulfstan. His chest was dark with blood which stained the end of his white beard. He supported himself with one elbow on the ground and his eyes were filled with hate. Roger de Mortimer joined the Duke, now King of England, and the two sat on their horses looking down at the old warrior, descended from Viking raiders and still full of their fierce spirit.

There was no fear, even now, in Wulfstan's eyes. He groped in his cloak, bloodying his hands in his own wounds as he did so and produced an amber ring. This he held up to the two Normans, and they blanched when they saw it. For this was the terrible ring used in pronouncing the curse of the Norse.

"May the death shrouds be dragged from your corpse, William of Normandy," Wulfstan said, "and may your bones be fed to the dogs in the streets. May your sons bring you sorrow and the air you breathe no health. . . ." The words of the Curse of the Ring rolled on into the silence, and neither William nor de Mortimer seemed capable of checking them. When they were finished, Wulfstan turned his face to the ground and died, and William pulled savagely at the reins of his charger and moved off, shaken.

It was the worst of bad beginnings. A savage hold had to be kept on the Saxons after this if the Conqueror was to keep his throne. They had to be forbidden to leave their homes at night and they had to be dispossessed of their lands. The task was not easy.

Almost as his first act, William, it is said, made Roger de Mortimer Lord High Constable to help him keep control of his new kingdom. The office was to become one of the most powerful in the land.

The Lord High Constable of England is one of the four great Officers of State who attend British monarchs at their coronations. In the time of Ralph de Mortimer and the Norman kings, his power extended not only over England but also into Normandy which, of course, was united with England then. His duties were chiefly of a military nature. He was in charge of the army under the king and, with the Earl Marshal, judged all matters of chivalry. He advised on tactics, said which barons should accompany the king to war, how many men they should bring with them and what part they should play in a campaign. In olden days, when no man was regarded as being of any worth unless he followed the profession of arms, the Lord High Constable was a man to be feared and envied.

The office was transmitted from father to son, from the time of William the Conqueror and for many centuries thereafter. It seems to have been transferred early in its history, however, from the de Mortimer family to the de Bohun's, another powerful Norman clan. The de Bohuns held the title until the male line of the family became extinct and only two daughters of the house remained. Both married into families of royal blood, the houses of Lancaster and Stafford. The Staffords then became the hereditary Lord High Constables of England.

However, the grim manner in which, according to the story, the office of Lord High Constable was created brought an equally grim ending to the last man to inherit the title. Maybe it was the curse of the old Thane of Wulfstan still at work. Certainly his curse seems to have been effective in the case of William the Conqueror. Centuries after William's death, his bones were exhumed from their resting place in the Abbey of Caen and scattered around the streets for stray dogs to gnaw upon. Nobody knows what became of them.

The last man to inherit the office of Lord High Constable of England was Edward Stafford, Duke of Buckingham. He quarrelled with Henry VIII over Cardinal Wolsey, who was the King's favorite at the time, and fell from royal favor. He was charged with treason, found guilty and beheaded on May 17, 1521.

Today, the office of Lord High Constable is revived only for coronations. It is usually bestowed on an outstanding soldier—the Duke of Wellington was Lord High Constable at the Coronation of Queen Victoria. His duties are little more than to attend the sovereign during the ceremony.

CHAPTER IX

The Steward, Chamberlain and Marshal

IN ADDITION to the Lord High Constable, three
other Officers of State serve the British monarch
at the coronation. Foremost among them is the Lord
High Steward, a man whose powers were so great in
earlier times that kings did all they could to abolish
the office. They feared, and not without grounds, that
the Lord High Steward might seek to displace them
on the throne.

The Lord High Steward's office dates from Saxon
times, long before William the Conqueror came to
England. Originally the title was Lord High Stead-
ward, meaning Ward of the King's Stead (or place),

and the man who filled the post was really the assistant king or queen. If the monarch were a minor, the Steward ruled for him. If he were out of the kingdom, away on war or on a visit to some other court on the European continent, then the Steward ran the country in his absence.

This, of course, made the kings uneasy. They did not like to leave their country to be run by another, however loyal he might seem to be, lest they come back and find their faithful Steward sitting on the throne in their place. The problem was solved, or rather an attempt was made to solve it, by giving the office to one family to be handed down from father to son. It was hoped that this would appease ambition.

Selected for this high trust was the Beaumont family to whom belonged the earldom of Leicester. All seems to have gone as well as could be expected until around 1230 A.D. when one Simon de Montfort succeeded to the title of Earl of Leicester and also that of Lord High Steward.

De Montfort was a deeply religious man who had taken part in a crusade to the Holy Land. He was also harsh and strait-laced. At this period in English history, the barons were seeking more power in the running of the land and more freedom from the whims and personal rule of Henry III. De Montfort, although loath to lose the favor of his sovereign, sided more and more with them. In the end, he led a revolt of the barons against the King, whom he defeated and took prisoner at the Battle of Lewes in 1264.

Thereupon, de Montfort set up a new parliament in which he gave increased representation to the barons and also to the townspeople. This made him popular with the townspeople. Of course, the barons didn't like it, for what they wanted was more authority for themselves and not for mere shopkeepers and merchants. Those barons who held lands on the Welsh borders and who were always the more warlike rose against de Montfort, and he was defeated and slain at the Battle of Evesham, in 1265. Some say he was merely wounded in the battle but, surrounded by his enemies, fell in a river and, because of the weight of his armor, could not get out and so was drowned. Whatever the true cause of his death, de Montfort was killed, and no king after that let the office of Lord High Steward get far outside the royal family. Henry III was persuaded to confer the title again but gave it to his own son, Edmund "Crouchback," who was Earl of Lancaster. The office remained in the royal family until it was given to the son of John of Gaunt, Duke of Lancaster, who became King Henry IV.

Henry IV was a wise king and a stern father. He sent his own son to jail for roistering and robbing people in the streets of London. In his wisdom he decided he would abolish the office of Lord High

Steward altogether and ruled that it should be revived only on very special occasions.

Today, the office is created only for coronations, and the order reinstituting it gives authority to the holder: "from the rising of the sun to the setting thereof." That in itself is sharp evidence of the fear in which former kings and queens held their Lord High Steward.

But "from the rising of the sun to the setting thereof," the power of the Lord High Steward is second to that of the sovereign himself. It is, of course, authority in name only, for the British people govern themselves through their parliament and their laws. However, in recognition of his high office, the Lord High Steward walks immediately before the monarch in the coronation procession and carries the Crown of England with which he or she is to be crowned.

The two other officers who serve at the coronation are the Earl Marshal of England and the Lord Great Chamberlain. They also have had their troubles and disagreements with former kings and queens, though not quite in the same way as did the Lord High Stewards.

The Lord Great Chamberlain, for instance, has the duty of waiting upon the monarch as a sort of personal valet. It used to be his task to bring the king his clothes on Coronation Day and help him dress in all the elaborate robes needed for the ceremony. He also took care of the king's bedchamber, guarded it on the night before the coronation and then at the coronation banquet which followed led the "service of ewry."

This is a strange way of saying that he served the king with water and a basin in which to wash his hands. Centuries ago, the "service of ewry" was very important, for there were no knives and forks or napkins. Instead, people cut the meat with their daggers and picked it up with their fingers to eat it. In return for providing the king with water and a basin, the Lord Great Chamberlain received the gold bowl in which the water was poured.

As payment for his services in the king's bedchamber, the Lord Great Chamberlain received a fee of forty yards of crimson velvet for his robe, the king's bed and bedding, his nightgown and all the furniture of the royal chamber where the king lay the night before his crowning, including the curtains, valances and other draperies. He was also entitled to the king's underclothing and all the clothes he wore before putting on his raiment for the coronation.

Today these fees sound strange indeed, but many centuries ago, good bedding, furniture and clothing were very expensive, as they still are. So the payment to the Lord Great Chamberlain was really in recompense for services rendered. This practice, unfortunately, led to trouble.

King James I, a Scotsman crowned King of England in 1603, refused point blank to be parted from his silk shirt, his stockings and so on. The Lord Great Chamberlain insisted that these articles were his by right. The King appealed to him on a man to man basis to forego them. The Lord Great Chamberlain said that it wasn't a question of man to man but king to chamberlain and he wanted the King's shirt. Eventually, the King persuaded the Chamberlain to accept the sum of two hundred pounds instead, and so King James I was able to keep his shirt, the first of the monarchs to achieve such a victory as far as is known.

An even more delicate situation arose in the case of Queen Anne, who was crowned a century later in 1702. She shut the door of the royal bedchamber firmly and said, tradition or no tradition, she was going to robe herself. The Lord Great Chamberlain, as became a gentleman, did not press the matter. However, there was still the question of his fee. He was entitled to receive the Queen's nightgown, her petticoats and other garments.

The matter was resolved with a great deal of nicety on both sides. Queen Anne kept her underclothing and the Lord Great Chamberlain received, instead, the sum of three hundred pounds. George I, crowned in 1714, paid three hundred and fifty pounds to retain his wardrobe. Today, however, all the Lord Great Chamberlain gets for his services is

his forty yards of crimson velvet from which to
make his robe for the coronation. The office of Lord
Great Chamberlain has belonged, since it was originated sometime in the twelfth century in the reign
of Henry I, to the de Vere family and is now held by
the Earl of Cholmondeley.

❖❖❖

The last of the Officers of State at the coronation
is the Earl Marshal, who has the most difficult job of
all to perform. Where the duties of others have
waned through the years, his have remained so extensive that he must have a staff of helpers.

Perhaps the Earl Marshal's foremost duty, from a
practical point of view, is carrying the Crown during
the coronation and assisting in placing it on the head
of the sovereign. (The Lord High Steward carries
the Crown in the procession which follows.) Once
there, a crown being somewhat heavy and clumsy to
wear, it has to be kept in position by the Marshal. In
doing this, he is permitted by tradition to hold the
Crown by the fleur-de-lis (or three-leaved lily) in
the front, and no one else is allowed to touch it at
that time.

It is related that during the Coronation of James
II, the last of the Stuart kings, the Crown almost top-
pled off the King's head to the ground. The Earl
Marshal of that day caught it in time and put it back
in place, whispering in the sovereign's ear a little
smugly, "This is not the first time that my family has

helped to keep the Crown on the King's head!"
James was duly gratified by this reminder of loyalty,
but he would not have been so pleased had he known
that the Earl Marshal was even then in correspond-
ence with William of Orange who was to displace
James on the throne a little later.

The Earl Marshal's duties do not end with keeping
the royal Crown in place. He must "appease and prevent all tumults and noises and disturbances in the
king's presence." He must see that all the doors to
the Abbey and Palace are guarded, with the exception of the door to the royal bedchamber—that being the duty of the Lord Great Chamberlain. He
must also keep the peace within seven miles of the
court.

For his services he used to receive the horse on
which the king rode to his coronation together with
its bridle, saddle and caparisons, the cloth from the
table on which the king dined at his coronation banquet, the Robe of Estate, which the king wore during the dinner and, as a special delicacy, the back-
bones with the adjoining meats of all swans and
cranes served at the banquet. Since a coronation banquet is no longer held and the sovereign now goes
to the coronation in a coach, the Earl Marshal has to
do without these fees today.

He was also entitled to receive fourpence for everyone committed to his custody by the High Steward on Coronation Day and all fines levied on of-

fenders on that day not amounting to more than three shillings and fourpence, about fifty cents now.

His most onerous duty, however, and one which he must still perform, is that of issuing orders to the peers attending the coronation regarding the robes they are to wear, the style of their coronets, the ornaments they may display and so on. These instructions are detailed and must be strictly observed.

Peers, for instance, on the Earl Marshal's order, must wear mantles of crimson velvet with a cape covered with *miniver,* a white fur. On the miniver are to be rows of ermine according to the rank of the nobleman involved. Barons must wear two rows of ermine, viscounts two, earls three, marquesses three and a half and dukes four rows.

The Earl Marshal must see that coronets are of silver gilt and that no jewels or precious stones are set in them. The coronets, like the capes of miniver, differ according to the degree of the noble wearing them. A baron, for example, must have on his coronet's rim six silver balls placed at equal distance from each other. A viscount must have eight silver balls raised on points, with four gold strawberry leaves and four more silver balls alternately between them. The coronet of a duke must have eight gold strawberry leaves around it.

Another matter to which the Earl Marshal must attend is the length of the train which the wives of the various nobles must wear. Years ago, when the length of the train was a sign of the degree of wealth and fashion of the owner, the ladies tried to outdo each other with longer and longer trains. The Earl Marshal was given the job of producing some kind of order out of the resulting chaos and set about it with manly determination and considerable efficiency. Now baronesses may have a train three feet long, viscountesses one of three feet three inches, countesses three feet six inches and marchionesses three feet and nine inches.

Having all this work to do, the Earl Marshal is provided with an extensive staff. He is given thirteen lieutenants, who are members of the ancient College of Arms. Each has his own title. There is Garter Principal King-of-Arms, Clarenceux King-of-Arms and Norroy King-of-Arms. Then come the six Royal Heralds, Windsor, Chester, Lancaster, York, Richmond and Somerset. Finally there are the four Pursuivants: Rouge Croix, Portcullis, Bluemantle and Rouge Dragon.

The present Earl Marshal of England is Bernard Marmaduke Fitzalan Howard, Sixteenth Duke of Norfolk. His duties are not confined to coronations, for he must also arrange state processions and ceremonials, royal marriages and funerals and attend the sovereign at the opening and closing of Parliament. He is the most indispensable man in the official life of the sovereign.

CHAPTER X

Claims to Service

MANY OTHERS, besides the four great Officers of State, are entitled to serve the British sovereign at the coronation. Some render the most peculiar of services such as supporting the monarch's arm when he receives the Royal Sceptre, or providing a red glove for him to wear on his right hand. Others have duties to perform which are no longer of any use and so have been dropped from the modern spectacle. Behind each one of these attentions offered the sovereign, there is an interesting and ancient story.

All have a common beginning in grants of lands or manors to favored individuals. The early kings, and foremost among them the great conqueror, William, Duke of Normandy, made it a practise to reward their followers with gifts of estates and castles. In doing this they also wanted to be sure that those who received such largesse would continue to be loyal to the throne. So grants of land were made on condition that a particular service was rendered to the sovereign, usually at his coronation. Such an arrangement is called grand serjeanty and constitutes a legal contract or obligation.

This system worked well enough when it was first introduced and where title to a particular property was clear. In the course of time, though, either through marriage or the extinction of a particular line, titles became clouded. Several people claimed the honor of performing one and the same service for the sovereign. So to rule on the conflicting claims, a court was set up which became known as the Court of Claims. This court has been called into session, in one form or another, for every coronation since that of Richard II in 1377. The last time it met was toward the end of 1952 to consider petitions connected with the Coronation of Elizabeth II.

Here are some of the rights in grand serjeanty upon which the Court of Claims has been asked to rule at one time or another.

The Dean and Chapter of Westminster claim the right to instruct the sovereign in the forms and ceremonies of the coronation and to assist the Archbishop of Canterbury at the service. They also treasure the privilege of keeping the robes and ornaments of the coronation and receiving "certain fees and allowances." These fees today consist of sums of money, although many years ago they included "one hundred simnels of bread (spiced cakes), a gallon of wine and as many fishes as became the royal dignity."

The Bishop of Durham and the Bishop of Bath and Wells have for centuries been permitted to stand one on the right and the other on the left of the sovereign and help him to his feet or ease him into the Coronation Chair as required. At each succeeding coronation for several hundred years, the bishops have claimed this privilege before the Court of Claims, and it has been upheld.

The Barons of the Cinque Ports insist that it is their duty to carry a canopy over the sovereign's head in the procession in Westminster Abbey. In recent years, a canopy has not been used because it interferes with the view, but the barons have been assigned a special station in the Abbey to show that they are not forgotten by their monarch.

There is an interesting story behind this particular service of the Barons of the Cinque Ports. *Cinque* is French for *five,* and originally five ports, Hastings, Romney, Hythe, Dover and Sandwich, all on the south coast of England, were given particular duties to the king, among them furnishing almost all the ships and men needed for the Royal Navy. In return they received certain maritime privileges. The barons are not really noblemen but the mayors, justices and members of Parliament elected from the five cities. In the thirteenth century, King John determined to make a passage across the English Channel from England to Normandy. The weather was foul with rainstorms and squalls of wind whipping the sea into foam, and the boat in which the King was to travel offered little protection. A number of merchants from the Cinque Ports accompanied the King on his voyage. Seeing their Sovereign seated on an open deck, with the rain beating down upon him, they obtained a piece of canvas from the sailors and held it over his head. All the way across the Channel, the loyal merchants sheltered the King. Ever since then, it has been the privilege of the Barons of the Cinque Ports to hold a covering over the sovereign's head at his coronation, or alternatively to have a place of honor at the ceremony.

The Earls of Erroll in Scotland, who are hereditary Lord High Constables of that country, lay claim to attend each coronation carrying a silver baton, weighing twelve ounces. This is tipped with gold at each end and has at one extremity the Royal Arms of England and at the other, the arms of the House of Erroll. The baton is the symbol of the Scottish Lord High Constable's office, and the claim dates from the time of Robert the Bruce, King of Scotland, who awarded the honor to the original holder because of the continued loyalty of the family.

One of the strangest privileges is that of the Lord of the Manor of Worksop. Title to the Manor was granted originally on condition that the head of the family provide a red glove for the king to wear on his right hand during the coronation. Why red is hard to say, but the glove made the carrying of the heavy Royal Sceptre at the ceremony a little less arduous a task for the monarch. The Lords of the Manor of Worksop have provided such a glove for the sovereign through several centuries and in return have continued to hold their hands.

Many similar services, once performed in return for title to estates, have fallen into disuse following the decision not to hold a Coronation Banquet. Such a feast has not been held for over a century, but if it were revived, then the services would have to be revived also. This would find the Lord of the Manor of Addington in Surrey looking up a recipe for a dish called dilligrout, which he must serve to the sovereign at the coronation feast. Just what dilligrout consists of is difficult to discover. The recipe is a secret one, held in the family, and the only comment ever made publicly on its taste came from King Charles II, who took a spoonful of the thick soup and stated emphatically that he didn't like it.

The Lord of the Manor of Nether Bilsington in

Kent would, if a banquet were held, be required to provide three maple cups for the monarch; and the Lord of the Manor of Lyston, to serve wafers made of sugar, almonds, ginger and saffron.

Here are some of the other duties of landowners which have become obsolete but can be revived at the will of the sovereign. The Lord of the Manor of Shipton Moyne holds his lands through serving as the royal chief larderer at the coronation feast. Ashill Manor in Norfolk is held in return for the tenant acting as Chief Napier, or looking after all the table linen at the banquet. As his fee, he was entitled to all the linen used—a particularly lucrative reward. The "Lord of the Isle and Castle of Pelham and the Serviory and Dominion of Man" (Man being an island off the English coast in the Irish Sea) was required at one time to provide the sovereign with two peregrine falcons on his Coronation Day. The last time the birds were presented was at the Coronation of George IV in 1821. Perhaps the most extraordinary service in grand serjeanty was that attached to the lands of Kepperton and Atterton, in Kent. These lands were granted on condition that the owner hold the king's head, should he ever go to sea and become seasick!

Some duties were required as the result of having a particular office rather than receiving a grant of land. For instance, there was the Hereditary Grand Almoner, an office given originally to the Beauchamp family and then to the Bedfords. His task was to collect all the scraps that remained over from the Coronation Banquet and distribute them to the poor, to visit sick people, widows and others in need and to remind the king to give alms to them. He also had to sell the monarch's cast-off clothing and see that the money was given to the poor. For these duties, he received a silver dish and "a fine linnen towel together with a tun of good wine."

Then there was the Royal Herb Strewer, charged with strewing herbs over the floor of the Abbey and the banquet hall. Sanitary facilities being rather primitive many years ago, the Royal Herb Strewer was a man of considerable importance. The King's Versifier, who is known today as the Poet Laureate, was given a hundred shillings a year to compose suitable verses for the coronation and other great occasions. Today the hundred shillings have become a hundred pounds. Many of the greatest of the English poets have held this office, including Spenser, Ben Jonson, Dryden, Wordsworth and Tennyson.

The list would not be complete without mentioning the King's Cock Crower, who, before the days of clocks, solemnly crowed the hour around the royal palace. The King's Cock Crower, such are the ravages of time, has not crowed a single hour since the reign of George I who was crowned in 1714. George was a German, with not a word of English to him—he conferred with his ministers in Latin. He knew noth-

ing of English ways when he came over from Han-
over, and it is related that he was dozing quietly in
the palace one evening shortly after his arrival,
when a man in satin breeches entered, bowed
solemnly and commenced to crow loudly at him like
a rooster devoured with zeal.

The King was sure he was at the mercy of a madman and rang for his chamberlain, who explained the
situation to him. The precise words the King used
in reply have been lost, but he ordered the Royal
Cock Crower out of the room and out of the royal
service. Since then there have been only clocks in
the royal palaces!

One ancient office still remains today, though in
different form. It is that of the King's Champion,
and the story of its origin is so remarkable that it
deserves a chapter of its own.

CHAPTER XI

The King's Champion

IN THE ROYAL banqueting hall on the night of December 25, 1066, the wine flowed freely and the minstrels, anxious to obtain the favor of the new King, played as if all life were a merry caper. Tumblers ran between the tables performing their tricks, sometimes leaping on them, the bright balls spinning merrily between their deft hands. The flames from a hundred torches splashed ruddy light on the crests of the nobles who were dining with the King, and from the rafters hung their banners, bright hued and proud.

Yet there was a note of strain in the air, an undercurrent of tenseness and anxiety, as if this was a celebration of people who might shortly find themselves not conquerors but captives. William, Duke of Normandy, who had been crowned King of England that day in Westminster Abbey, slouched in his chair, moody and unmoved by the laughter and jesting around him.

The bloody fight with the Saxons after the coronation still preyed on his mind. He could not get rid of the feeling that at any moment his new subjects might rise against him again and snatch away the crown so recently placed upon his head.

It was true that there were a thousand or more men-at-arms on guard outside to prevent surprise, but they were little enough protection against a population that hated William and all he stood for. When the King thought of these things, neither the playing of the minstrels nor the tricks of the tumblers could shake his gloom.

Suddenly in the midst of the false merriment there came a thunderous knocking on the double door of the banqueting hall. This was followed by the sound of a brief, sharp struggle and the doors were flung open by a mounted knight, completely armed, who rode his charger full tilt down the stone floor, scattering guests, servants, minstrels and tumblers in all directions.

The horseman pulled up within a few feet of the King's chair and flung a glove of chain mail on the floor—the ancient gesture of challenge to combat.

William half rose, and the horseman cried in a loud voice in Norman French, "Oyez! Oyez! If there be any person, of whatever estate or degree he be, that will say or prove that William, Duke of Normandy, is not the rightful King of England, then here am I to say that he lies and to challenge him to combat on behalf of my Lord and Sovereign!"

All the music and jesting had now ceased and nothing was to be heard but the spluttering of the torches and the clinking of chain mail as men-at-arms and knights turned round to see who the horseman was. No one spoke a word or made any move to accept the challenge. It was William himself who broke the silence.

"Sir Knight," he said, "who are you who speaks so boldly? All are Normans here. Do you bear the same challenge to the Saxons who growl about us?"

"I am Robert de Marmion of the Barony of Fontenay, Champions to the Dukes of Normandy," the knight replied, "and in keeping with my ancient position, I challenge all of your enemies, Sire, whether Saxon or Norman or of any other nation, to contest your right to the throne."

"Then shall you be rewarded," said William, "and rewarded as boldly as the challenge you have made. Now hear me, all present. To Robert de Marmion of the Barony of Fontenay, I, William, Duke of Normandy and King of England, shall give such lands as he may wish, to be held by him and his descendants for all time, in return for which he and they shall serve as Champions to the Kings of England, defying their enemies to do battle with them should they wish to contest their title to the throne."

Thus the office of King's Champion was inaugurated in England—and it has existed to this day (see plate VII).

The lands which Robert de Marmion obtained in return for defying the enemies of William the Conqueror were Tamworth Castle in Leicestershire and the Manor of Scrivelsby in Lincolnshire. In return for these the heads of the house of Marmion continued to make this challenge at each subsequent coronation until the year 1291.

At that time, the last male of the house Philip Marmion died. He left, however, two daughters—both of whom were named Jane. The first married one Alexander de Freville and received title to Tamworth Castle. The other inherited the Manor of Scrivelsby as her portion of her father's estate. It was to the latter's descendants, after she also married, that the title of King's Champion passed on, though the de Frevilles contested the matter.

The family name changed from Marmion to Dymoke through marriage, but the Dymokes have been the King's Champions through the intervening centuries. However, it is a hundred and thirty-two years since they performed their original function in the way in which it was initiated. Up to the Coronation of George IV, in 1821, the challenge was given with all its ancient intent and ritual. The Champion, mounted on a white charger and clad from head to foot in armor, knocked on the door of the banqueting hall after the coronation and entered, accompanied by a herald and two squires. On his right was the Earl Marshal of England and on his left the Lord High Constable.

He repeated his challenge three times—once at the entrance to the hall, once in the center and once before the dais on which the King was seated. On on each occasion he threw his steel gauntlet on the ground, and the words of the challenge are given as these: "If there be any manner of man, of whatever estate, degree, or condition, soever he be that will say and maintain that our Sovereign Lord King this day here present is not the rightful and undoubted inheritor to the Imperial Crown of this realm, that of right he ought not to be crowned King, here is his champion who saith that he lieth and is a false traitor. And I am ready to maintain with him while I have breath in my body, either now at this time, or any whensoever it shall please the King's Highness to appoint—and therefore I cast down my gage."

In all the hundreds of years that it was given, the challenge has never been taken up, a remarkable circumstance since many kings of England had serious rivals to their crowns. Perhaps any potential

challenger did not think he had much chance of survival even if he won the encounter with the King's
Champion. For without followers he could not ex-
pect to hold the throne, and, even if widely supported, his best chance lay not in single combat but
in revolution—bloody or otherwise.

There were occasions, however, when the challenge was followed by the same hushed expectancy
as greeted it in the time of William the Conqueror.
When George III was crowned King of England,
rumors were widespread that the descendants of the
dethroned Stuarts were intent upon overthrowing
George and regaining the crown. On this occasion,
as the Champion issued his challenge, the guests
eyed each other, wondering whether one of their
number would accept it on behalf of the Stuart
"Pretender" as he was called. Another time, when
Richard III was crowned in 1483, with the boy-king,
Edward V, held prisoner in the Tower of London,
there were many nobles present who secretly supported Edward against the man who was usurping
his throne. None of them, however, picked up the
gage of the King's Champion to contest the matter.

At his coronation, George IV, a high-living, flam-
boyant and unpopular monarch, ordered that every
ritual and ceremony be observed. Afterwards there
was much criticism of the expense involved, and the
Coronation Banquet at which the Champion made
his appearance was dropped. There is another more

potent explanation, however, why this particular ceremony in its original form was eliminated from the coronation spectacle.

The right of trial by combat is part of the old Norman law. Indeed, it is part of the ancient law of many European countries, and stems from the belief that God will not permit innocence to be overcome by evil, even in physical combat. Thus, a man accused of a crime could challenge his accuser to battle. If he lost the encounter, he was executed out of hand. But if he won, he was deemed innocent and set free.

From this custom arose the practice of permitting a champion to fight on behalf of either party. However, the champion was allowed to take the side of the accused only if the latter were a woman, an elderly or infirm man, or a boy. Later kings and nobles were permitted to have champions fight for them, and had anyone accepted the challenge of the King's Champion, he would have had a strong claim to the throne, for the combat constituted a legal trial.

This fact was lost sight of for many years, and the law of trial by combat remained on the statute books of England for centuries. Then, in 1818, a case arose which awoke the whole nation to the dangers of such an arrangement. In that year, a man named Abraham Thornton was accused of murder. The evidence against him was heavy and his prospects of convincing a jury of his innocence appeared slight indeed. Pondering what he should do, Thornton stumbled across the fact that he need not go before a judge and jury at all but could demand trial by combat. That is just what he did.

He insisted upon meeting his accuser in mortal combat, and his request shook the law libraries of England to their dusty foundations. Search as they might, the legal experts could find no way of denying Thornton the right to maintain his innocence in a fight to the death. Someone, then, had to be found to fight him, and that proved an impossible task. The best attorneys in the land, willing to risk their legal reputations on the case, were not ready to hazard their lives. In the end Thornton was set free and the right to trial by combat deleted from the statute books of England.

This repeal of the law made a mere ritual of the function of the King's Champion. Today, the Champion, instead of issuing a challenge on behalf of the monarch, has the right to carry the Standard of England in the coronation procession. The privilege belongs now to Captain John Lindley Marmion Dymoke, Lord of the Manor of Scrivelsby, and a direct descendant of the champions of former kings and queens of England.

CHAPTER XII

Gold Stick and Silver Stick

IN THE YEAR 1660 the great experiment of an
England without a king had failed. It had come
to an end with the death of Oliver Cromwell, one of
its originators and its guiding genius. The people
who had fought so long and so hard for their rights,
who had sacrificed so much of their blood and their
treasure found themselves in a political vacuum.
There was no government other than that which
came from the surviving generals of Cromwell's New
Model Army. There was no constitution and indeed
no regularly elected parliament. So the people,
searching for guidance, decided that they must have
a king again.

They sent, then, for Charles Stuart, the son of Charles I who had been beheaded at the close of the English Civil War and asked him to return to England and take the throne. Thus Charles Stuart, who was to become Charles II, agreed to accept the crown. He had, however, some reservations, and, in view of the execution of his father, they were not unnatural. First, he desired a personal guard, a private army, for he was convinced that had his father had such a force at his disposal he would never have been overthrown and beheaded. So when he arrived at Dover on May 26, 1660, a troop of eighty cavaliers under the command of Lord Gerard of Brandon was there to meet him and escort him to the royal palace at Whitehall.

Next, he wanted the New Model Army of Cromwell's disbanded. Made up of farmers and merchants, of clerks and accountants, it had become the finest fighting force in all Europe. Nevertheless, by means of special taxes, the army was paid off in February, 1661, and dissolved.

Back in London, Charles pressed ahead with his plan for having an army that belonged solely to the king. The eighty cavaliers who escorted him from Dover he formed into the Royal Life Guards. Later he added to them another troop of horse raised by the Earl of Oxford, called the Horse Guards, or Blues, because they wore blue tunics. Collectively, the two groups became known as the Household

Cavalry, specifically charged with guarding the life of the sovereign. They were not long in proving their worth.

A year after Charles had returned to his throne and denuded London of all troops but his own, a wine merchant named Thomas Venner, who belonged to a revolutionary sect called the Fifth Monarchists, made an attempt to seize the city, burn down the palace and kill the King. The Household Cavalry was ordered to deal with the situation, and after some rioting and bloodshed, Venner was captured and the revolt quelled.

The Venner Riots, as they became known, set the King to thinking more about his personal safety. He decided that a captain of the Life Guards should be constantly in attendance on him to prevent an attempt at assassination. The trouble was that a determined murderer might pose as a captain in the Guards, obtain admission to the sovereign's presence and dispose of him. So King Charles ordered that the captain assigned to protect him should carry an ebony staff with a gold head, engraved with the Royal Cypher and Crown. A second officer, carrying a similar staff but with a silver head, was also ordered to hold himself in readiness to relieve the first.

One or the other of the two was to remain with the king wherever he might be, even standing guard outside the royal bedchamber. And today these two officers, members of the Household Cavalry, are still part of the royal household and their titles, Gold Stick in Waiting and Silver Stick in Waiting, are derived from the staffs which they carry. They attend the sovereign at all times and stand close to him or her at the Coronation Ceremony.

The two divisions of the Household Cavalry who accompany the monarch to and from the coronation and indeed at all formal appearances wear some-what different uniforms. These uniforms now seem more suited to ceremonial parades than battle, but they were devised originally to serve the sternest of purposes.

Both the Horse Guards and the Life Guards wear high jack boots which come well above the knee. These were originally designed to protect the thighs from lance and sabre thrusts, for in the days of cavalry charges, a man could readily be unhorsed and killed if wounded in the upper leg. Breastplates also are worn—again a survival of the days of cavalry fighting.

The Life Guards wear scarlet tunics with blue collars and cuffs; the Royal Horse Guards, blue tunics with scarlet collars and cuffs. Red was once regarded as the best color for a soldier's uniform, because blood would not show up against it. Thus, in battle, men were not demoralized by seeing their comrades wounded around them. Each member of the regiment has a plume on the top of his steel hel-

met, white for the Life Guards and red for the Horse
Guards or Blues. The different colors were used in
former times to distinguish the men in battle so that
the commander could readily tell where each regiment was. The plumes are made of spun whalebone
or yak's hair. But since yak's hair is becoming hard
to obtain, and whales are no longer readily found,
nylon may soon be used as a substitute.

The Household Cavalry also wear white bando-
leers (a belt slung over the shoulder to carry car-
tridges) with a small red cord down the center. The
red cord is nothing but decoration now, but once it
had a real use. After the monarchy had been restored
in England, many kings and queens were somewhat
nervous about the temper of the people. When they
rode through the streets of London in the royal
coach, they were surrounded by a troop of the Household Cavalry. Furthermore, the door to the coach
was locked to prevent anyone who might break
through the escort from dragging the sovereign out
and wounding or killing him. The key to the door
of the royal coach was hung upon this red cord.

Besides the Household Cavalry, five regiments of
Foot Guards also protect the sovereign and the several royal palaces which are scattered through London and its environs. These, with their bearskin
headdresses, their red tunics and dark blue trousers
with a red stripe down the sides, are familiar to
people in many parts of the world who have never

been to London. They have become the prototype of
the toy soldier. Their drill is so perfect that when
they are on sentry duty, you may watch them for
several minutes without seeing them blink an eye.

The five regiments are the Welsh, Scots and Irish
Guards, made up of men from each of these countries, the Coldstream Guards and the Grenadier
Guards. The Coldstream Guards date back to the
year 1660 when General Monk, in charge of an army
in Scotland, crossed the River Tweed at a village,
called Coldstream, to restore Charles II to the throne.
For this service, Monk's troops were not disbanded
by Charles but were attached to what he hoped would
become his private army.

The Grenadier Guards are not grenadiers at all.
They got their name when, at the Battle of Waterloo, their regiment stormed the positions occupied
by Napoleon's famous grenadiers and either killed
them all or took them prisoner. It was during the
same campaign that they also received a sharp rebuke
from the Duke of Wellington. The officers, the story
goes, were excessively proud of their uniforms which
they kept spotless and well pressed even in the front
lines. One day, during an action, a group of them
were standing together, oblivious to the enemy
fire, when it began to rain. Each, anxious that his
uniform should not become wet, raised an umbrella
to protect it. When Wellington heard of the incident,
he issued a sharp order positively prohibiting offi-

cers of the Guards from waving umbrellas in the face of the enemy!

It is only fair to add that the Royal Guards, whether the Household Cavalry or the five regiments of Foot Guards, can boast of battle honors desperately won in many campaigns all over the world. They were at Dunkirk, at Ypres and Mons, at Waterloo and El Alamein, and the tradition in the British Army is that the Guards never retreat. They either hold their ground or die.

CHAPTER XIII

The Royal Heralds

WITHIN the Kingdom of England there is a shadow realm, with three kings and ten nobles. It is a kingdom of which the British peoples become aware only at coronations or at the time of the death of their sovereign. Perhaps it would be better to say that this is a kingdom of reflection rather than of shadow. For it is composed of the Heralds of England, and heralds have no substance in themselves. They are merely images of the monarch. They do not, in their official capacities, speak for themselves nor live for themselves, but all their actions and words are those of the sovereign who is their master.

They have fine titles these Heralds, ringing of the days of armored knights and tournaments, of sorties from beleagured cities and of passages-at-arms with lance or mace or battle-axe.

First, there is Garter Principal King-of-Arms, the chief of all the Heralds, who takes his name from one of the noblest of the orders of knighthood—the Order of the Garter. That order came into being in the time of Edward III who, according to the story, was dancing at a banquet with the Countess of Salisbury. The Countess' garter slipped to the floor, bringing a few titters from the courtiers. The King picked it up and returned it to her, saying in rebuke to the sniggerers, "Honi soit qui mal y pense"—Norman French for, "Disgraced be he who thinks ill of it." From this incident originated, as a degree of knighthood, the Order of the Garter.

After Garter Principal King-of-Arms comes Norroy King-of-Arms, whose heraldic jurisdiction, laid down for hundreds of years, is north of the River Trent. And south of the River Trent, Clarenceux King-of-Arms holds sway.

These are the three kings of the mirror kingdom. They wear their own crowns—a circlet of gold with oak leaves around it. And when a new king-of-arms was appointed, he used, in olden days, to undergo a coronation of his own in imitation of his master. Wine was poured upon his head, he was invested with his tabard, or loose-sleeved coat, which is emblazoned with the badge of his office, and then the crown was placed upon his head.

Under the three Kings-of-Arms come the Heralds, who with the Pursuivants are the nobles of this kingdom within a kingdom. There are six English Heralds, each of whom takes his title from an historically important area in England. First, there is Windsor, then Chester, then Lancaster, York, Richmond and Somerset. Then come the Pursuivants, who are attendants upon the Heralds. These have the finest names of all—Bluemantle, Rouge Croix, Rouge Dragon and Portcullis.

At the present time the duties of the Kings-of-Arms, Heralds, and Pursuivants have been largely reduced to reading to the people official proclamations concerning the monarch—such as the death of the king, the accession of a new king, the appointment of a Court of Claims to hear petitions of service at the coronation and so on. They also form the staff of an institution called the College of Heralds, which keeps the records of the titled families of Britain. They trace back the ancestry of an applicant to see whether he is entitled to a badge or a degree of nobility, and they are recognized as the final authorities on crests and other heraldic devices. When a new noble is created, they supply him with a coat of arms in keeping with his rank and will instruct him on his privileges and duties. These, however, are merely the husks of what was once their service.

For in the thirteenth and fourteenth centuries, when heraldry was at its prime in England, the herald was the voice of the king or the noble who was his master. He declared war on his behalf, or sued for a truce. He regulated the tournaments between knights, inspected the arms used to see that they were correct, and saw that the chivalry of the joust was attended to in all its splendor and detail.

The person of the herald was sacred. Who touched him touched his master. Who killed him invited his own death in retribution. And so on the field of Agincourt, before the battle, Henry V sent Leopard Herald, his personal emissary, through the French lines to the Dauphin of France, quite sure that he would not be harmed in any way.

Another duty of the Heralds was to make a list of the knights, nobles and men-at-arms who fell in battle. To do this, they had to be able to recognize a fallen man from his coat of arms. And with hundreds of coats of arms in use, many of them differing only slightly one from the other, it took the greatest skill to make a correct report of the slain.

At the Battle of Evesham in 1265, when Simon de Montfort made his stand against the forces of the King and the barons of the Welsh border, it was his herald (who was also his barber) who told him who was taking the field against him. De Montfort was expecting to join forces with an army led by his son. He sent his herald to a high point of ground to read the banners of the knights as they came near, emerging from the distance in the morning mist. When the herald read out the banners, de Montfort knew that it was not his son's army but the King's that was approaching and that all was lost.

The mirror kingdom of the Heralds has its own language which consists partly of words and partly of pictures. A gold lion on a red background means just a coat of arms to most people. But to the herald it signifies the house of the Earl of Arundel, whose coat of arms it is. In his language it is described as *gules, a lion or*. Thus, the language of the kingdom of heralds was devised to describe and record the different coats of arms in exact terms so that there could be no misunderstanding them.

It is a fascinating tongue, with a hint of romance in every word. A band drawn through the middle of a shield and occupying about one third of the total area is called a fesse. A line running diagonally across is a baston. A V-shaped line is a chevron (from which we get the name for the stripes of a non-commissioned officer today). In all there are ten or so different kinds of lines—engrailed, embattled, indented, invected, undy, nebuly, dancetty, raguly, potenté, dovetailed and urdy. You may rest assured that if a new kind of line is produced in the world, it will be the invention of a herald.

Then there are the colors used in blazoning a coat of arms or a shield of arms. (The two are the same except that one was displayed on the coat which a knight carried over his armor and the other on his shield.) Gules stands for the color red; vert, green; azure, blue; sable, black; or, gold; argent, silver.

The Heralds showed their greatest ingenuity, however, in creating designs, or insignia, for coats of arms (the heraldic name is *charges*). The first charge used seems to have been a cross, for knighthood and Christianity were closely linked. A red cross displayed on a shield or a coat of arms usually meant that the owner had taken part in one of the crusades in the Holy Land. Later, though, all kinds of crosses were used, and even with this one symbol, it was possible to devise coats of arms for scores of families. The Royal Pursuivant, who is called Rouge Croix, has a red cross on his coat as the name implies.

After the cross, pictures of animals were used. The lion was well known even as far back as the twelfth and thirteenth centuries. A lion lying down was said to be *couchant*. Looking over his shoulder he was *regardant*. In the act of walking he was *passant*, and with his paws raised in the air as if attacking his prey, *rampant*.

This provided a great deal of scope for the Heralds and they improved upon nature's lion by devising animals with two tails and two heads. After the lion came the leopard, but here the early Heralds ran into difficulties. Some people had been as far afield as India and tropical Africa and had seen leopards.

Left. *The Crown of King Edward the Confessor with which all British Monarchs have been crowned. Although destroyed in Cromwell's time, a faithful copy was made from the original specifications on the order of Charles II.*

Right. *The Imperial State Crown. This is the Crown worn by the British Monarchs on state occasions. It contains among many fabulous gems the Black Prince's Ruby, a sapphire from the ring of Edward the Confessor and the second Star of Africa, cut from the Cullinan diamond.*

PLATE IX

PLATE X

Top Left.   *The Ampulla and the Anointing Spoon.*
Top Right. *The head of the Royal Sceptre.*
Bottom.   *The Two Royal Orbs.*

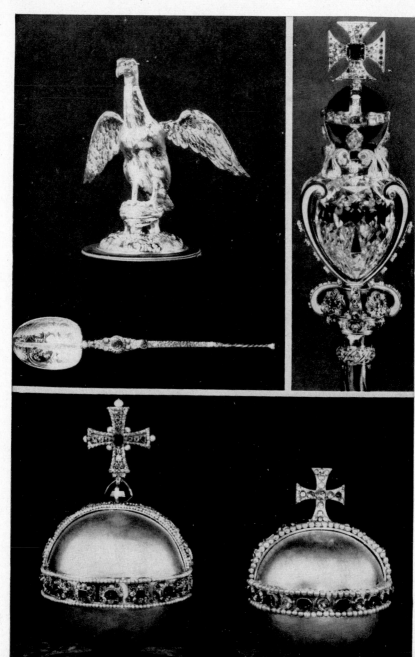

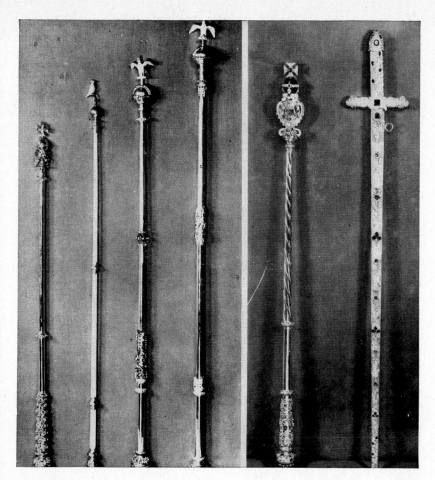

Left.   *The four Royal Sceptres.*

Right. *The Royal Sceptre, which contains the Great Star of Africa cut from the Cullinan diamond and weighing 516½ carats.*

The Jewelled State Sword, the most valuable and beautiful in the world, made of Damascus steel and covered with diamonds, rubies, sapphires and other gems.

PLATE XI

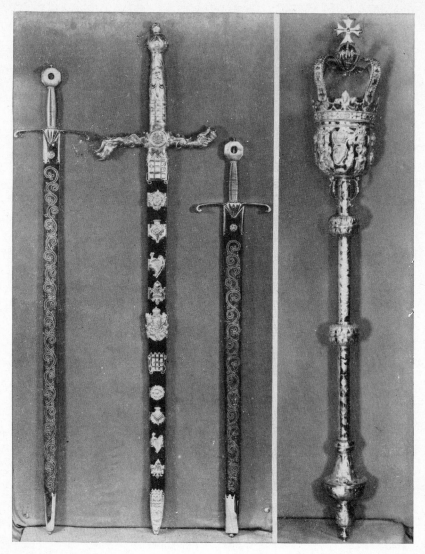

Left. *The three State Swords—the Sword of Spiritual Justice, the Great Sword of State and the Curtana Sword of Mercy. The scabbard of the Sword of State is decorated with designs of the rose, the thistle and the shamrock set in precious stones.*

Right. *The Mace carried by the Sergeant-at-Arms.*

PLATE XII

However, the leopard was to most an unknown beast. In the books on heraldry the leopard was described as having the body of a cub lion and another animal called a pard. So the heralds decided the leopard would look something like a lion and something like a pard. But what did a pard look like? No one knew. Thus the leopard was made to look like a lion except that its head was always shown full face. A full-faced lion on anyone's coat of arms is, therefore, a leopard!

After the leopard, there appeared the tiger. He was more difficult still. Practically nobody in the days when heraldry was at its prime had seen a tiger. Hence, the tiger came to have a head like a wolf's and a body that looked something like a lion's (or a leopard's) but tufted with hair to show that it was really a tiger.

Side by side with the animals that were known to exist, the Heralds used other animals that were thought to exist. They were, of course, all mythical. But it was some hundreds of years, however, before people were prepared to admit that there was not, in the whole length and breadth of the world, a white horse with a single spiralled horn in the center of its head called a unicorn.

The griffon was one of the earliest of the imaginary animals developed for heraldry. He had the hind parts of a lion and the rest of him was all eagle—beak, wings and claws. Griffons were almost always rampant—that is to say, reared up on their lion's legs ready to attack with their eagle's beak and claws. Then came the wyvern. He was a small winged dragon and seems to have been related in some way to a real dragon. The arms of Sir Francis Drake bore a dragon, for the name Drake is derived from a Greek word meaning dragon.

Birds, fish, dogs, deer, flowers, leaves—a great variety of natural objects—all became the subjects of charges on coats of arms. Thus it is a tribute to the skill of the herald that with such a wide variety of heraldic devices he could, almost at a glance, tell who was the wearer of a particular coat and whether he was the head of the family, or the first, second, or third son and so on.

Once all the great nobles had their heralds. But as their powers declined and their private armies were disbanded, only the Royal Heralds remained, and they survive to this day. Besides the English Royal Heralds there is also a Herald of Scotland, Lyon King-of-Arms, and of Northern Ireland, Ulster King-of-Arms.

These then, together with Garter Principal King-of-Arms, dressed in their loose-sleeved cloaks, which have remained unchanged for many centuries, attend British monarchs at their coronations as the representatives of a kingdom within a kingdom whose functions have long since dwindled almost to nothing.

PART V

Westminster Abbey in which British Monarchs are crowned and the Coach in which they ride to their Coronations

CHAPTER XIV

Westminster Abbey

THE CHURCH in which British monarchs are crowned is Westminster Abbey. If all else in England were destroyed and only Westminster remained, much of the nation's history could still be readily traced. For Westminster Abbey is the greatest of the English national monuments. It has seen her kings and queens crowned for nine hundred years. It is the final resting place of many of them. Every stone in its walls and floors contains a story as moving as any romance ever written. To stand in Westminster Abbey is to stand in time and see the record of a nation unfold before you.

Nobody knows who laid the first stone of this great

church. There are many theories, some provable. There is also a legend which is unbelievable, except that many believe it.

The legend says that Westminster was built as a church of much smaller size by St. Mellitus who was the first Bishop of London and who came to England from Rome in or around 604 A.D. The church was built on the site of the present Abbey which is near the River Thames and adjacent to the Houses of Parliament in the heart of London. In those days, however, the ground about was marshy and the site was a small island called Thorney.

When the church was completed, St. Mellitus, according to the story, set a date for the consecration, and crowds of Saxons gathered around the day before to be sure to be on hand for the event. They put up tents of skins for themselves on the land nearby, for they did not want to spend the night on the island of Thorney. Late in the evening of the day before the consecration, a fisherman was approached by an elderly stranger who asked if he would ferry him over to the church on the island. Although the fisherman was dubious, there was something reassuring about the stranger's manner. He not only was quiet and gentle, but he also spoke familiarly of fishing as if he himself in his youth had followed the sea and the waters.

So the fisherman put his doubts aside and rowed the stranger over to the island. Then his passenger asked if he would wait a little and carry him back again and, when this was agreed, set off towards the church. It was now getting quite dark. The mists rolled up out of the river and across the island. There was no moon and only a winking star or two to keep the fisherman company. Even the fires of the Saxons across the river were not able to penetrate the thickening mist and the fisherman grew lonely. Not wanting to leave his boat with the tide rising, he nevertheless set off to find the stranger and tell him they had better be getting back.

Then, as swift as the dawn, the darkness was dispelled by a glorious light, and the air was filled with the sound of such singing as the fisherman had never heard before. All around the church there appeared a host of people in glittering garments, some carrying tapers and others crucibles filled with incense. They went through the ceremony of consecrating the church while the fisherman hid in a clump of willows, very much afraid, and watched them. Then, as suddenly as they had come, the glittering host disappeared. The mist and darkness returned, and the stranger came towards the fisherman who asked him, fearful of what his answer might be, who he was and what he had done.

"I am a fisherman like you," the stranger replied, "and my name is Peter. I knew the Christ for whom this church is raised, and He has sent me to consecrate it. Go to Bishop Mellitus in the morning and tell him the church is already blessed, and that all may now celebrate divine service there."

The fisherman, despite what he had seen, could not believe that he stood in the presence of the chief apostle. So the stranger said that as proof of the consecration Bishop Mellitus would find a cross cut in the new stone of the building. "I will give you one more sign," he added, "the same that was given to me when I doubted also. Throw your net into the water and raise it."

This the fisherman did, and it came up heavy with glittering salmon.

"Take the best of these fish and give them to the Bishop," Peter commanded. "Tell him what I have said and he will believe you." Then he walked away through the mist and was gone. The fisherman did as he had been bidden, and the cross of consecration was found newly cut in the stone of the church. From that day on, for centuries later, one tenth of the salmon caught in the Thames within the limits of London was brought to the church. And in honor of the visit of Peter, the fisherman to bring in the first fish of the season and offer it on the high altar was feasted in the church hall.

That is the legend, and although it is supposed to have occurred thirteen hundred and more years ago, Westminster Abbey is still called by some the Church of St. Peter.

The Abbey of today, as distinct from the church

which occupied the site for some centuries before
and around which the legend of St. Peter grew, was
built by Edward the Confessor and then rebuilt by
Henry III in 1245.

Edward was one of the saintliest of the early English kings, devoting more time to religion than to the
affairs of government. The exact date of his birth is
not easy to establish, but it seems to have been at
the dawn of the eleventh century. His father, Aethel-
red II, fled England where his rule had been unpopular, and so Edward was brought up at the Norman court on the European continent. While in exile, he vowed that he would make a pilgrimage to
Rome, but he was never able to achieve his purpose.
Consequently, when as a grown man he was recalled
to England to succeed to the throne, he decided
that instead he would erect a large minster or church
to the glory of God.

The minster, built in a few years on the Isle of
Thorney, was Westminster Abbey in its first identifi-
able form. A date was set for the dedication of the
Abbey and the nobility and clergy of England were
summoned to attend the ceremony as, centuries before, the Saxons had gathered for the dedication
of the earlier church. Suddenly Edward's health
failed and he knew that he would not live long
enough to see the work consecrated which he had
planned to be the crowning achievement of his life.

He, therefore, advanced the date of the consecration and there was just time for it to be held when he died on January 5, 1066. It is not even certain that he was able to witness the ceremony. Some authorities say he did and others that he didn't. Nevertheless, in recognition of his saintly character Edward was buried in his own Abbey before the main altar. Thus when, some few months later, William the Conqueror was crowned King of England in the Abbey, his mailed feet were squarely placed over Edward's tombstone.

Since then, every sovereign of England has been crowned at Westminster Abbey, with the exception of Edward V and Edward VIII, now Duke of Windsor, who were not crowned at all. This makes an almost unbroken series of coronations for nine centuries. Edward V was a boy-king, caught in a struggle for power between two uncles, and from his story stemmed many a tale of a boy and his wicked uncle. He lived from 1470 to 1483. When he ascended the throne, one of his relatives, commonly called his uncle, Richard, Duke of Gloucester, had him committed to the Tower of London under the pretext that he was to be kept there for safety until his coronation could be arranged. The boy-king, never suspecting the fate that lay ahead for him, complained of being lonely, and the uncle arranged for his younger brother, the Duke of York who was only ten, to be put in the Tower with him. The two were never seen alive again, and the uncle himself was crowned King, to become Richard III.

What happened to the two children remained a mystery for nearly two hundred years. Then workmen, making some repairs in the Tower of London, came across a wooden chest buried under a staircase. Inside they found the bones of two boys of about the age of the two princes.

In 1933 Professor William Wright, President of the Anatomical Society of Great Britain and Ireland, examined the bones, which had been interred in Westminster Abbey. He came to the conclusion that they were the remains of two youths aged between twelve and thirteen. Since the condition of one of the skulls suggested suffocation, an earlier story that the two princes had been suffocated in their sleep received a measure of confirmation.

Not only is Westminster Abbey the coronation place of British monarchs but it is also the last resting place of many of them. Indeed, the great Abbey is full of the tombs of those who by their lives forged the history of Britain. One may wander through it, stepping as it were from one century into another, past warrior and poet, wit and statesman, and hear in the mind's ear the shouts of those who stood for liberty, the angry words that led to great campaigns and battles, the clicking of the beads of long dead monks and the ringing of broadswords on shields and armor.

Among the tombs there is first the shrine of Edward the Confessor himself, which is in a chapel of its own at the back of the high altar before which the coronations are held. Originally his body had been laid to rest in the floor of the Abbey. Thirty-six years after his death, Gilbert, Abbot of the Abbey, commanded the grave to be opened. When the monks pulled the covering stone aside, there was not the slightest sign of decay about the remains! The grave was closed again and two hundred years later, on October 13, 1269, the body of Edward the Confessor was placed in its present tomb.

Nearby is a double shrine, that of Richard II (1367-1400) and his first wife, Anne of Bohemia, whom he loved so deeply that when she died he became insane. In the bottom of the Queen's tomb, some openings were originally left through which the grief-stricken King presumably could put his hand to touch her coffin. These have now been closed up. Atop the shrine, with a look of great peace upon their faces, are the figures of the two lying side by side. Richard himself had the effigies made and by his orders the hands were entwined so that all who saw them in the centuries to follow would know how much he had loved his Queen. The unhappy King was not to have even that testament to his devotion left. Vandals, many years later, removed the entwined hands. In 1400 Richard died in Pontefract Castle in Yorkshire after resigning his throne, five years after the death of his wife. Around his story Shakespeare, nearly two hundred years later, wrote his tragedy *King Richard II*.

Not completely in the Chapel of the Confessor, but in a sort of smaller chapel of its own called a chantry, is the tomb of Henry V. It was he who at Agincourt in 1415, with six thousand archers, a thousand men-at-arms and a few thousand other foot soldiers, all weak with dysentery and near starvation, challenged and defeated a French force four times his number. The English lost in this engagement only thirteen men-at-arms and one hundred infantry; the French five thousand, most of them of noble birth.

Henry died in France, probably of dysentery, and his funeral was the most splendid held in the Abbey up to that time. The body was escorted by six hundred knights in black armor, their lances reversed. Behind, on a chariot, lay an effigy of the King made of cuir-bouilli—that is, leather soaked in boiling water and pressed over the features so as to take their form. The art of making this kind of death mask, which was painted to flesh tones, has long since been lost. Thousands of white-clad priests followed behind, each carrying a torch, and with these was a score or more knights with torches also. The hearse was drawn by six horses, each bearing a separate coat of arms—those of Normandy, of King Arthur, of Edward the Confessor, of St. George and of

Henry himself, combining the Royal Arms of France, which he had conquered, with those of England, of which he was King.

Borne also in the funeral cortege were Henry's saddle and shield and the helmet which he had worn at Agincourt. These were put on a crossbeam of the Abbey. The torches filled the vaulted ceilings with flickering light, and the voices of the choir swelled around the shrines of other kings less glorious. In the throng stood many of the bowmen of England who had fought with Henry at Agincourt and whom he had called not subjects but brothers on that valiant day. It is said that they wept for they loved him.

In Westminster, one may see now the saddle, the shield and the helmet of Henry V, still hung upon the crossbeam where they were put on the day of his funeral. The bright colors of heraldry have faded from the shield. The banners he carried are but pale cobwebs of cloth, but in the helmet, mute evidence of the struggle, there is a heavy dent received from the mace of a French knight at Agincourt on St. Crispin's Day of 1415.

Not far from the tomb of Henry V there is another monument. It is the grave of Britain's Unknown Soldier, who died at a place unmarked and on a day unrecorded in World War I; one of over nine hundred thousand of the men of Britain, her Empire and her Commonwealth, who fell in that struggle.

In the scope of a chapter or even a book it is not

possible to describe the nobility and beauty of Westminster Abbey, the stone pendants that drip from
the ceiling as if they were of lace, the lithe arches
that vault towards the sky, the quiet crypts and the
solemn columns gentled by time. For here is everything of England that is brave and generous of heart.
And it is not dust, but living memory.

CHAPTER XV

The Royal Coach

FOR ALMOST two hundred years, British kings and queens have gone to their coronations in a splendid coach which is so heavily decorated that it is believed to be the most magnificent ever built. It must be said, however, that although it is so beautiful, it is also very uncomfortable. Queen Victoria refused to use it during the latter part of her reign, and other kings and queens have complained that they were jolted heavily when travelling in this Royal State Coach, as it is called.

The Coach was designed in 1761 by Sir William Chambers, who was one of the most prominent architects in England and built many of the public buildings in London. With the exception of the door panels, the vehicle is gilt all over, including the wheels and the pole by which it is pulled along. Rolling down the street behind a team of eight horses, it looks like a carriage of solid gold. Eight horses are rather a large number for pulling a coach in which only three or four people are sitting, but when Sir William designed the vehicle he was concerned more with splendor than efficiency. After the Coach was finished, it was found to weigh four tons, largely because of its lavish decorations. Each horse then must pull the equivalent of half a ton of coach —and that is without any passengers at all.

This huge weight is what makes the Coach so uncomfortable to travel in, for no method of providing springs has been satisfactorily worked out. Instead, the body is supported by stout leather braces which absorb some of the shock but permit the seating compartment to sway around. Thus riding in the Royal State Coach is quite unpleasant. It is rather like being on a ship and rolling with the waves.

On the front and back of the Coach, between the wheels are four gilded tritons, or sea gods. The driver's seat is between the two in front, and these are represented as drawing the Coach along by cables over their shoulders. At the same time they hold sounding shells to their mouths, announcing the approach of the monarch of the sea. The two figures on the rear of the Coach carry fasces. These are ancient emblems of authority, originating in Roman times, and consist of bundles of sticks with an axe in the middle of them. Since, on the Royal State Coach, the fasces are held by sea gods, the axe has been replaced by a trident, or three-pronged harpoon. The board on which the coachman rests his feet is a large golden scallop shell, decorated with carvings of marine plants. The pole by which the carriage is pulled represents a bundle of lances, and the wheels are copied from those of the ancient triumphal chariots of Rome. Spokes, rims and hubs are elaborately carved.

The body of the vehicle is made up of eight carved palm trees and the branches support the roof. The four trees making the corners are hung with representations of trophies won by Britain in early wars. On the centre of the roof are statues of three boys, representing England, Scotland and Ireland. They support a crown and carry other symbols of royalty. The side panels carry paintings by Giovanni Battista Cipriani, a classical Italian painter and engraver who was a friend of Sir William Chambers, and the seat linings are of scarlet velvet.

A coach of such a size as this—it is twenty-four feet long and eight feet three inches wide—takes a great deal of skill to drive through the streets. Weighing so much, if it were to get out of hand in going down a hill, it could cause serious injury or even death not only to the sovereign but possibly to many bystanders. For this reason, four men, called postillions, ride the four left-hand horses, and these are really the drivers. No coachman is used during the coronation parade.

Queen Elizabeth I is believed to have been the first of the English monarchs to have gone to her coronation in a coach, or chariot as it was called then. Others had gone on horseback, and her departure from custom created a sensation. Soon many of the nobles had ordered coaches for themselves and their wives, and although the roads were very bad, the style became popular. In those days, the main thoroughfare through London was not a highway but the River Thames, and people travelled from one part of the city to another in their private barges, which were beautifully decorated. The Queen's introduction of a coach spelled the end of the bargeman's career, and many pitched battles were fought between bargemen and coachmen as each sought to put the other out of business. Barges gave way to coaches in the end, of course, but British sovereigns still have in their service a Royal Bargemaster, although his position is purely nominal.

PART VI

*How the first Queen Elizabeth went
to her Coronation; a description of
the Regalia which is now used &
the Coronation Ceremony &
the Homage which follows*

<hr/>

CHAPTER XVI

The First Elizabeth

WHEN the first Elizabeth was crowned Sovereign of England November 17, 1558, the nation was determined that the occasion would be marked by display and pageantry such as had never been seen before. The land, under the rule of her half sister, Queen Mary, had been fouled and torn by religious prosecution. It was hoped that the new Queen would bring unity, peace and prosperity to the troubled kingdom. So the greatest celebration was arranged. And it would be no exaggeration to say that the show put on in the streets of London rivalled that of the Coronation itself in Westminster Abbey.

The merchants and the different trade guilds crammed the River Thames from the Tower of London to Westminster with barges brightly painted and gilded, and decorated with brave streamers and flags. Some had companies of musicians aboard, others guns of different sizes which were discharged to send their thunder rumbling over the ancient river and rattling through the narrow streets that crowded down to it. From all over England, writers and musicians had been brought to London to compose songs and verses in honor of the Queen. There has probably never been a coronation before or since so well commemorated in words and music. Along the route which the Queen and her coach were to take from the Tower to the Abbey, the streets had been converted into highways of splendor, decorated with cloth of gold and drapes of crimson velvet, and alive with flags and bunting. At different places, tableaux had been arranged to represent various aspects of the history of England and the basic rules for governing the nation. This was an era in which such stage display was brought to its greatest eminence, paving the way for the dramatists Marlowe, Shakespeare and Ben Jonson.

The great men who were to step forward later in her reign to bring glory and renown to England were but boys when the first Elizabeth set out in her coach for her crowning. Francis Drake, who later sailed around the world, was a lad of fourteen being educated in Kent by his kinsman, Sir John Hawkins. Perhaps he came to London to see his Queen on the way to her Coronation, wearing a borrowed sword and a borrowed cloak, for there was little money in his family. Walter Raleigh was a boy of seven, living in a Devon farmhouse. Before him lay a brilliant career as statesman, chemist, explorer, navigator, colonist, poet, ship designer and historian.

Elizabeth was twenty-six when she was crowned, a year younger than the present Queen. She had never thought to accede to the throne, being the third in line of succession. Neither did the present Queen Elizabeth, who at the time of the death of King George V was also third in line to the throne. Perhaps because she was so inexperienced, perhaps because the times were so uncertain, perhaps because they sympathized with this young woman whose father had had six wives and whose mother had been executed, the people of England were utterly determined to do all they could to make the first Elizabeth's reign a success. They did not hesitate to offer her advice along with their demonstrations of loyalty and love. This advice they gave indirectly, in the form of the tableaux which they erected all along the route of her Coronation procession.

Thus, when the Queen left the Tower of London in her coach, surrounded by nobles on horseback and with the Heralds of England walking ahead of her, she had gone but a few yards when she came to an

arch, erected across the street. On top of this stood
a beautiful woman, representing the people of London, to bid her welcome to the city. Further along, at
the entrance to Gracechurch Street, there was another display. Again an arch had been thrown across
the road, and on this were three stages, one above
the other. On one was a figure representing her
grandfather, King Henry VII; on another, her father Henry VIII and Anne Boleyn, Elizabeth's
mother who had been beheaded; and on the third,
an actor representing Elizabeth herself. The meaning
was plain to all—that however unhappy her background might have been, she was Royal England,
the descendant of Royal England, and her people
would support and serve her as such. A child read
an address to the Queen explaining the meaning of
the piece and then the procession moved on through
streets festooned with chains of cloth of gold and
flowers, velvet and silks, while gallants and merchants, seamen, burghers and yeomen cried their al-
legiance to the Sovereign.

At one point an elderly woman, poorly dressed,
who had no other gift to offer, pushed her way
through the nobles surrounding the Royal Coach and
gave the Queen a garland of rosemary. The story of
this rosemary has lasted throughout the intervening
centuries. For the Queen would not be parted from
it and carried the fragrant herb close to her throughout the procession to the very steps of Westminster.

Rosemary is for remembrance, and although the first Elizabeth had many faults, she had an overwhelming love for the common people. So she kept the gift of rosemary, cherishing it above all the other gifts that were showered upon her, to show that she would keep faith with her people. Years later, when the army raised by the people of London to repel an expected Spanish invasion gathered at Tilbury, the Queen appeared on a palfrey, wearing a breastplate of steel and with a drawn sword in her hand. She said then that though she was but a woman, yet she had the spirit of a man and would fight like one for her country. Many who saw her, cobblers and vintners, woolen merchants and shipbuilders, remembered the rosemary of her Coronation and knew that she had not forgotten her people and never would.

The procession continued then, with at almost every turn an elaborate stage presentation. At Cornhill was an overhead platform showing four gates with the Royal Throne above them. The piece was called "The Seat of Worthy Governance" and the figure of the Queen was shown supported by the virtues Prudence, Justice, Fortitude and Temperance. At their feet lay Superstition, Folly, Bribery and Rebellion. Further on, another display illustrated the nine Beatitudes; another, the picture of a decayed and flourishing kingdom and here the Queen was given a Bible by a figure representing Truth.

At Fleet Street were four stages, one above the

other. Actors on three of them represented the three classes of the kingdom—the common people, the clergy and the nobility. On the topmost platform was a figure depicting Deborah of biblical times, who had been the restorer of the House of Israel and had ruled wisely over her people for forty years. When the procession left the City of London proper to enter the City of Westminster, for London then, as now, is a composite of many self-governing communities, a child bade her farewell. The Queen answered in a voice heard clearly by all who pressed around, "Be ye well assured I shall stand you a good Queen." It was a promise which she fulfilled gloriously in a reign that lasted just over the forty years of Deborah's.

The first Elizabeth's reign, opening with such pageantry, brought great achievements and fame to England. With another Elizabeth on the throne, Britons everywhere are hoping that the glories of an earlier era will be duplicated. Times have changed but not so very greatly. There is now, as there was then, a need for trade, for a strong currency, for peace and for a common effort to put the country on its feet. The first Elizabethans solved their problems successfully. The twentieth-century Elizabethans have great expectations for their future too.

CHAPTER XVII

The Regalia

MORE than a crown is required to make a monarch. Also needed for the Coronation of the Sovereign of Great Britain are a pair of Golden Spurs, five Swords, an Orb, a Ring and two Sceptres. Each one has its own name and significance and all together they are called the Regalia.

The value of these pieces in terms of money runs into many millions of dollars. They have, however, another kind of value which has no relation to money, for these exotic things are all of them symbols—mute and lifeless as all symbols are, but nonetheless sacred to the people of Britain because of their significance. Their inner meaning has remained unchanged for a full ten centuries, so that there is almost something magical about them when their symbolism has weathered the assaults of time and the changing of the world for so long.

These, then, are the pieces of the British Regalia— what they are and what they represent.

First, there is the Coronation Crown, itself, called the Crown of Edward the Confessor. Edward was crowned with the original crown in 1043 A.D., more than four centuries before the discovery of the New World. The same crown continued to be used until it was melted down and sold in 1649 after the English Civil War, as already related. The present Crown was made for the Coronation of Charles II in 1662 and is a faithful copy of Edward's original one. This is the most important item in the Regalia and is about as big as a size seven-and-a-half hat, weighing over five pounds. The Crown consists of a circlet of gold, decorated with rosettes of precious stones around which there are circles of diamonds. From its rim arise four fleurs-de-lis with four crosses placed one each between them. The fleurs-de-lis and the crosses are studded with diamonds. Over the top of the Crown are two arches of gold, crossing each other, and above these, where they meet in the center, is a golden ball surmounted by a cross.

The Crown of Edward the Confessor is the Crown of the kingdom, but Britain is more than a kingdom; it is also an empire. Symbolizing this fact, a second

crown is used at the Coronation. After the Crown
of Edward the Confessor has been put on the head
of the monarch by the Archbishop of Canterbury, it
is taken off and replaced by another which the sovereign wears during the procession that follows. This
second crown is called the Imperial State Crown and
was made for the Coronation of Queen Victoria in
1838. The Imperial State Crown is admitted to be the
most valuable and beautiful in the world. It consists
of diamonds, pearls, rubies, sapphires, and emeralds
—a cascade of precious stones—set in solid gold and
silver. Inside is a crimson velvet cap, trimmed with
ermine and lined with silk. At the front, in the center of a huge cross studded with diamonds, is the
famous Ruby of the Black Prince, the story of which
has already been told. Three other crosses form the
main ornaments around the rim of the Crown. Each
has an emerald in its center and is composed of diamonds. Between these crosses are the four fleurs-de-
lis, for the Imperial State Crown is modelled on that
of Edward the Confessor. The fleurs-de-lis have rubies
in their centers, and to enhance the color of the
rubies, the rest of the design is filled in with rose
diamonds. Also the two arches rising over the top of
the Crown contain well over a thousand diamonds.

Besides the Black Prince's Ruby, the Imperial
State Crown contains a huge diamond cut from
the Cullinan, a great sapphire from the Crown of
Charles II, the pearl ear-drops worn by the first

Queen Elizabeth, and a sapphire taken from the Coronation Ring of Edward the Confessor. In all, apart from the bigger stones, there are in the Imperial State Crown four rubies, eleven emeralds, sixteen sapphires, two hundred and seventy-seven pearls and two thousand seven hundred and eighty-three diamonds. Indeed, when the Crown was made more than a century ago, it proved so splendid and so valuable that Parliament passed a law forbidding it to be taken out of England for any reason at all.

The actual crowning of the monarch in Westminster Abbey is the culminating part of the Coronation Service. The other pieces of the Regalia, which are used earlier in the ceremony, are as follows: First, there are the Golden Spurs of St. George, which are touched to the heels of the monarch as a sign of his or her knighthood. The primary duty of a knight being the protection of the weak, this ceremony reminds the sovereign that as a knight he must help those who are in need of aid. The Spurs, when they have been touched to the ruler's heels, are put upon the altar and redeemed later by the payment of a fee. This custom dates from an old law which required an armed knight on entering a church to give his spurs to the clergy, thus surrendering the symbol of his knighthood in the presence of his Creator. He got them back later on payment of a fee called Spur Money, used for charitable purposes.

After the Ceremony of the Spurs, the Jewelled

PLATE XIII

King George VI with Princess Elizabeth at Windsor, 1946.

King George VI inspecting the Yeomen of the Guard, who still wear the Tudor uniforms designed for them during the reign of Edward VI.

PLATE XIV

The Royal Family at Balmoral Castle.

Queen Elizabeth with her consort, the Duke of Edinburgh. Photo was taken in the drawing room of Clarence House by Baron.

PLATE XV

Queen Elizabeth taking the salute at the Trooping the Color Ceremony.
PLATE XVI

Sword of State is girded around the monarch's waist by the Archbishop with the charge that it be used to defend the right, protect the Church, the poor and the helpless. The sovereign immediately takes the Sword off and places it upon the altar signifying that the full power of the throne will be used in the defense of the Church.

The Jewelled Sword of State, sometimes called the Sovereign's Sword, was made for the Coronation of George IV in 1821. At the head of the hilt is a large diamond with rubies on four sides, and below along the hilt are rows of emeralds and diamonds. The scabbard is of dull gold encrusted with jewels and carries the emblems of the Rose of England, the Thistle of Scotland and the Shamrock of Ireland. This magnificent blade is used during the Coronation instead of the Great Sword of State, which is a huge weapon with a hilt so big that it must be held in both hands. The Great Sword of State is carried before the sovereign on all official occasions, but is too cumbersome to be girded on the monarch during his or her crowning. Nonetheless, the Great Sword of State is the official sword of England.

Three other swords form part of the Regalia, each with their own significance. These are the Swords of Spiritual Justice and Temporal Justice, which pledge the sovereign to fair dealing in both religious and civic affairs. Finally, there is a curious blade called Curtana. This is a sword from which the point has been clipped off. Curtana is the Sword of Mercy. The blunted end pledges that justice will not be harsh but clemency will be shown by the sovereign to his people whenever it is justified.

The next part of the Regalia used is the Orb or Globe. This is a strange piece, six inches in diameter, consisting of a ball of gold, decorated with diamonds, emeralds, rubies and sapphires. On top is a large cut amethyst that supports a cross one and a half inches high, so that altogether the Orb is eleven inches tall. The Orb can be traced back as a symbol to Roman times, for many of the Roman rulers carried such an insignia to show that they ruled the known world. Nowadays, the Orb is placed in the right hand of the monarch; and the cross surmounting it signifies the domination of Christ over the earth.

Then comes the Coronation Ring, which is also called the Wedding Ring of England. It is put on the fourth finger of the right hand of the sovereign by the Archbishop as a seal on the promise that all the duties undertaken by the monarch will be attended to. Then the Sceptre with the Cross is given the ruler by the Archbishop. It is probably the most splendid sceptre in the world. It is made of solid gold and is two feet nine and a quarter inches in length. In its head is the huge Star of Africa diamond, cut from the Cullinan. This stone weighs five hundred and sixteen and one-half carats, more than four times the weight of any other cut diamond in the world. Atop this massive stone is a cross. Another sceptre, the Sceptre with the Dove, which is also called the Rod of Equity and Mercy, is next placed in the sovereign's left hand by the Archbishop. It is somewhat shorter than the first, being two feet and seven inches in length and is adorned with diamonds. On a mound at the top is a golden dove with wings outstretched. The Sceptre with the Dove pledges equal justice and mercy to all subjects.

The Regalia is kept in the Jewel Room of the Tower of London, where it may be seen by the public, for it belongs to the people of Britain and is not the personal property of the British monarch. The night before the Coronation the Regalia is taken from the Tower and lodged in the Jerusalem Chamber of Westminster Abbey. On the morning of the Coronation it is brought from here in solemn procession and placed upon the high altar of the Abbey for the ceremony.

CHAPTER XVIII

*The Coronation Ceremony**

NOTE—during the following description the word *king* is used to designate the monarch rather than the double term *king or queen.*

A LL THE NOBLES of the realm gather on Coronation Day in Westminster Abbey for the
anointing and crowning of the sovereign. There are
the Lord Great Chamberlain, the Lord High Steward, the Lord High Constable and the Kings-of-
Arms of England, Scotland and Northern Ireland.
There are the dukes and marquesses and their la-

---

* Readers may be interested to check this description with an
outline of the events of the Coronation of George VI in 1937
which follows in the Appendix.

dies, clad in their robes of crimson velvet and the knights and pages.

The sovereign is met, on arrival at the Abbey, by the Earl Marshal, and is preceded into the church by a procession of the clergy and nobles, the latter carrying the Regalia. As the monarch enters the church, the choir of Westminster sings Psalm CXXII which opens with the words: *"I was glad when they said unto me, let us go into the house of the Lord. . . ."* The sovereign then kneels in prayer on a stool before the high altar, afterwards standing beside the Chair of State on the right. This Chair of State is not a throne but a royal seat, for the sovereign does not sit upon the throne until crowned.

The first part of the Coronation Ceremony consists of the Act of Recognition. The Archbishop of Canterbury, escorted by Garter Principal King-of-Arms, the Lord Chancellor, the Lord Great Chamberlain, the Lord High Constable and the Earl Marshal, goes to the east, south, west and north sides of the area before the altar and calls out to the assembled people: "Sirs, I here present unto you [name of the monarch] your undoubted sovereign: Wherefore all you who are come this day to do your homage and service, are you willing to do the same?" As this is done, the monarch must turn to face the section addressed so that they may recognize him. And each division of the congregation replies, in answer to the Archbishop's question: "God Save the King!" These

shouted replies in the Act of Recognition were because of the riot and bloodshed during the Coronation of William the Conqueror.

Then the lords, who have carried the Regalia from
the Jerusalem Chamber, pass it to the Archbishop
to be placed upon the altar. Only the swords are
retained, as custom does not require them to be
handed over to the Archbishop at this time.

Next comes the Coronation Oath. This is adminis-
tered by the Archbishop to the monarch in this
form: "Will you solemnly promise and swear to govern the peoples of Great Britain, Northern Ireland,
Canada, Australia, New Zealand, the Union of South
Africa, of your possessions and other territories to
any of them belonging or pertaining according to
their respective laws and customs?" To this the sovereign must reply: "I solemnly promise to do so."

"Will you to your power cause law and justice in
mercy to be executed in all your judgments?" is the
next charge, to which the answer is, "I will."

"Will you," the Archbishop continues, "to the utmost of your power maintain the laws of God and
the true profession of the Gospel? Will you to the
utmost of your power maintain in the United Kingdom the Protestant Reformed Religion established
by law? And will you maintain and preserve inviola-
bly the settlement of the Church of England and the
doctrine, worship, discipline and government thereof

as by law established in England? And will you preserve unto the bishops and clergy of England, and to
the churches there committed to their charge, all
such rights and privileges as by law do or shall ap-
pertain to them, or any of them?"

To this the reply is given: "All this I promise to
do."

The sovereign then goes to the altar, escorted by
the Lord Great Chamberlain, and kneels on the
steps. The Archbishop brings an open Bible, on
which the king puts his right hand and says aloud:
"The things which I have here before promised, I
will perform and keep, so help me God." He then
kisses the Bible and signs his name to the oath taken
and returns to the Chair of State. Here the sovereign repeats the words of a declaration, drawn up by
Parliament, in which he promises to rule according
to the laws of the land.

Then starts the communion service during which
comes the most sacred part of the ceremony, the
Anointing of the Monarch, consecrating him to God.
This commences with a hymn and then a prayer by
the Archbishop calling on the Almighty to ". . . bless
and sanctify thy chosen servant [name of sovereign]
who by our office and ministry is now to be anointed
with this oil, and consecrated king; strengthen him,
O Lord, with the Holy Ghost and Comforter; confirm and establish him with Thy free and princely

spirit, the spirit of wisdom and government, the spirit of counsel and ghostly strength, the spirit of knowledge and true Godliness. . . ."

The sovereign then rises from the Chair of State and, with the assistance of the Lord Great Chamberlain, removes his crimson outer robe, and the Cap of State, a cap of red velvet, trimmed with ermine, which is worn as a head covering before the crown is officially bestowed. He then sits in the ancient King Edward's Chair, with the famous Stone of Scone beneath. Four Knights of the Garter hold a pall of silk over his head. The Dean of Westminster takes the Ampulla, containing the anointing oil, and pours some into the Anointing Spoon, and the Archbishop of Canterbury anoints the monarch on hands, breast and head saying, when finished: "As Solomon was anointed king by Zadok, the priest, and Nathan, the prophet, so be you anointed, blessed and consecrated king over the peoples whom the Lord Your God hath given you to rule and govern."

The sovereign next kneels on a footstool before the Chair of King Edward to receive the blessing of the Archbishop which is as follows: "Our Lord Jesus Christ, the Son of God, who by His Father was anointed with the oil of gladness above His fellows, by His holy anointing pour down upon your head and prosper the works of your hands, that by the assistance of His heavenly grace you may preserve the people committed to your charge in wealth, peace and godliness; and after a long and glorious course of ruling a temporal kingdom wisely, justly and religiously, you may at last be made partaker of an eternal kingdom, through Jesus Christ our Lord. Amen."

At this point, the king becomes a person with a dual character; not only a civil authority, but also a cleric of the church. And to acknowledge this change, he is clothed in a strange outer robe called the Colobium Sindonis. This corresponds, in part, to the alb of a bishop. It is a sleeveless garment of fine soft linen, edged in lace, with a lace flounce, nine inches deep at the bottom. It is open at the sides and gathered in at the waist. Over this is put the Close Pall or Supertunica, another garment like an alb, but made of cloth of gold and having wide sleeves.

The sovereign sits again in the Chair of King Edward for the Ceremony of the Spurs. The Lord Great Chamberlain receives these from the Dean of Westminster, who takes them from the altar where they have lain, and touches them to the king's heels as a token of knighthood. The Spurs are immediately returned to the altar to be redeemed later by payment of Spur Money.

The Ceremony of the Sword follows next. The Great Sword of State which has been carried before the sovereign is placed for the time being behind the high altar in the Chapel of the Confessor.

It is replaced by the Sword of Justice Spiritual, which is blessed by the Archbishop of Canterbury with these words: "Hear our prayers, O Lord, we beseech Thee, and so direct and support Thy servant [name of sovereign] who is now to be girt with this sword, that he may not bear it in vain; but may use it as the minister of God for the terror and punishment of evil-doers, and for the protection and encouragements of those that do well . . ."

The Sword is then delivered to the king by the Archbishop with the injunction: "Receive this kingly sword, brought now from the altar of God, and delivered to you by the hands of us the bishops and servants of God, though unworthy." The king now stands and the Lord Great Chamberlain girds the Sword on him while the Archbishop says: "With this Sword do justice, stop the growth of iniquity, protect the holy church of God, help and defend widows and orphans, restore the things that are gone to decay, maintain the things that are restored, punish and reform what is amiss and confirm what is in good order. . . ."

The monarch then takes the Sword off and returns it to the Archbishop as a pledge that he will use it as asked. The Sword is redeemed later by payment of a hundred shillings to the Dean of Westminster and carried in the Coronation Procession which follows.

The robing of the sovereign in the vestments both of a cleric of the church and the ruler of his realm is then continued. First, the Stole or Armill, a long narrow strip of cloth, is put around his neck. Then the Lord Great Chamberlain clothes him in the Imperial Mantle, which is shaped somewhat like a bishop's cope, the only difference being that it is square, whereas the cope is rounded. The four corners of the Imperial Mantle represent the corners of the earth over which rules the Divine King by whose virtue the monarch is crowned. Woven into the fabric are golden eagles, representing the British Empire.

When the robing is completed, the monarch sits again in the Chair of King Edward to receive from the Archbishop the other parts of the Regalia. To begin with, the Orb is placed in his right hand, with the exhortation that "when you see this Orb thus set under the Cross, remember that the whole world is subject to the power and empire of Christ, our Redeemer." The king gives the Orb back to the Dean of Canterbury to be put on the altar again. Later he carries it in the procession from the Abbey. Then the Coronation Ring is placed on the fourth finger of the right hand as the "ensign of kingly dignity."

The Lord of the Manor of Worksop, holding his lands as a result of this service, now gives the Archbishop a red glove for the right hand of the king who puts it on. Next comes the presentation of the two sceptres, the Royal Sceptre (or Sceptre with the Cross) which is put in the king's right hand by the

Archbishop and the Rod of Equity (or Sceptre with the Dove) which is placed in the left hand. On giving the Sceptre with the Cross the Archbishop says: "Receive the Royal Sceptre, the ensign of kingly power and justice." This is possibly the shortest exhortation of the whole ceremony, though it involves the one symbol which, together with the Crown, is essential to the royal authority. However, the whole of the Coronation Ceremony places its stress not upon power but on mercy, justice and wisdom. So when the Rod of Equity is presented, the admonition of the Archbishop is more weighty. He says, "Receive the Rod of Equity and Mercy; and God from whom all holy desires, all good counsels and all just works do proceed, direct and assist you in the administration and exercise of all those powers which He hath given you. Be so merciful that you be not too remiss; so execute justice that you forget not mercy. Punish the wicked, protect and cherish the just and lead your people in the way wherein they should go."

Now comes the final act of the Coronation, the placing of the Crown of Edward the Confessor upon the head of the monarch. It is for Britons everywhere the most solemn and moving moment of the whole ceremony. The Archbishop holds the Crown before the altar and says, "O God, the crown of the faithful: Bless we beseech Thee and sanctify this, Thy servant [name of monarch] and as Thou dost this day set a crown of pure gold upon his head, so enrich his royal heart with Thine abundant grace, and crown him with all princely virtues, through the King eternal, Jesus Christ our Lord. Amen."

No words are spoken at the actual crowning. The Archbishop of Canterbury comes from the altar, accompanied by the Archbishop of York and the Bishops of Durham and Bath and Wells. The Dean of Westminster carries the Crown on a cushion of cloth of gold. When they have come before the sovereign, he bows his head, and the Archbishop of Canterbury takes the Crown, raises it up high, and slowly lowers it upon the head of the king. At that moment, all inside the Abbey leap to their feet and cry "God Save the King!" in acclamation of their sovereign. There is a flourish of trumpets and a flash of gold as on every side barons, marquesses and other nobles put on their own coronets. Outside the Abbey, at Tower Hill at Windsor and at Hyde Park, guns thunder a royal salute to the newly crowned monarch, and their cannonade, carried by radio and television, is heard all over the world to tell British peoples everywhere that their sovereign is crowned.

When the acclamation inside the Abbey has ceased, the Archbishop of Canterbury says, "God crown you with a crown of glory and righteousness, that by the ministry of our benediction, having a right faith and manifold fruit of good works, you may obtain the crown of an everlasting kingdom by the gift of Him whose kingdom endureth forever. Amen." Then, following the presentation of a Bible as "the most valuable thing that this world affords," and the benediction service, interrupted for the Coronation Ceremony, is continued.

Here the actual Coronation Ceremony ends. Two final acts remain: the seating of the newly crowned monarch upon the throne and the rendering of homage by his people.

CHAPTER XIX

Homage and Fealty

Note—as in the preceding chapter *king* is used to designate the monarch, whether king or queen.

IT IS still the custom for a British monarch to be lifted bodily onto his throne by princes of the Church and the nobles of his realm. This ceremony dates back to the time when the Celtic chiefs were raised upon their shields and carried before their people as related in the first chapter. The throne is placed on a dais behind the Chair of King Edward in which the actual crowning takes place. The king goes to the throne after the benediction and is lifted into it by the archbishops, bishops and nobles who have attended him. When he is seated in it, they gather around him and the Archbishop of Canterbury says: "Stand firm and hold fast from henceforth the seat and state of royal and imperial dignity, which is this day delivered unto you, in the name and by the authority of Almighty God, and by the hands of us the bishops and servants of God, though unworthy: And as you see us to approach nearer to God's altar, so vouchsafe the more graciously to continue to us your royal favor and protection. And the Lord God Almighty, whose ministers we are, and the stewards of His mysteries, establish your throne in righteousness, that it may stand fast for ever more, like as the sun before Him, and as the faithful witness in Heaven. Amen."

Then follow the Act of Homage and the Oath of Fealty. There is a difference between the two. In paying homage, the subject places his hands between those of his sovereign as a sign of submission to him. He then recites the Oath of Fealty which is one of service. To save time, these are no longer done individually. The oath is repeated in chorus, with the principal cleric or noble of the group kneeling before the throne and paying homage for himself and the others by putting his hands between those of the monarch.

The Archbishop of Canterbury is the first to give homage, and the rest of the clergy join with him as he kneels before the throne and says: "I [each gives his own name] will be faithful and true and

faith and truth will bear unto you our Sovereign
Lord, and your heirs Kings of Great Britain, Ireland
and the British Dominions beyond the Seas, Defenders of the Faith. And I will do and truly acknowledge the service of the lands which I claim to hold
of you, as in right of the Church. So help me God."
The Archbishop then kisses the sovereign on his left
cheek—an ancient form of sealing an oath. Next to
pay homage and take the oath are the princes of the
blood—members of the royal family. They perform
the Act of Homage individually, each kneeling before the king, placing their hands between his and
saying: "I [name] do become your liege man of life
and limb and of earthly worship and faith and truth
I will bear unto you, to live and die, against all manner of folks. So help me God." Each kisses the sovereign on the cheek and touches the Crown as a further
pledge and acknowledgment of sovereignty. Then
follow the dukes and marquesses, earls, viscounts
and barons.

And when the homage is over there is a rolling of
drums, a flourish of trumpets and all in the Abbey
cry out: "God Save the King! Long Live the King!
May the King live forever!"

APPENDIX

AN OUTLINE OF THE

Coronation of King George VI

MAY 12, 1937

NOTE: *To guide readers through the form of the Coronation Ceremony, a summary of the Coronation of King George VI, taken from English newspaper accounts of the time, has been included. It is believed that the general order of events will remain the same for the Coronation of Elizabeth II and subsequent British sovereigns.*

I. The King and Queen rode to Westminster Abbey in the State Coach.

II. They were received by the Earl Marshal at the west door of the Abbey.

III. A solemn procession called "the Great Proceeding" escorted the King and Queen into the Abbey. In it were the Archbishops of Canterbury and York, the Bishop of Durham, the Bishop of Bath and Wells (a joint see), the Bishops of London and

Winchester, the Dean and prebendaries of Westminster, the Prime Minister and the Dominion pre-
miers. Added to these were the Officers of State bearing the Queen's Regalia, and all the great nobles and
heralds of the land.

IV. The Queen went in the forepart of this procession and was followed by the King surrounded by
his State Officers and their pages. Three of the
Swords of State, including Curtana, were carried before him. Their Majesties proceeded up to the nave
to a platform called "The Theatre." This extended
from the choir stalls to the high altar in the Sanctuary. The Coronation Chair with the Stone of Scone
beneath stood before the altar. Behind on a dais were
the two thrones. These were not occupied until the
crowning had taken place. The King and Queen sat
in two Chairs of State on the south side of the Sanctuary as the Ceremony commenced. Two faldstools
for kneeling on were placed before these. A third
faldstool was put before the Coronation Chair.

V. The seating arrangement of the assemblage in
the Abbey was generally as follows:

The members of the Royal Family, that is to say
the immediate family with the exception of the
King's sons (in this case, none), were seated in a box
to the right of the altar.

Peers of the realm were seated in the south transept
which gives off from the right of the Sanctuary.

Peeresses were seated in the north transept to the left.

Before the south transept chairs were placed in which Princes of the Blood (the Dukes of Gloucester and Kent and Prince Arthur of Connaught) were seated.

Members of Parliament were seated behind the peers and peeresses in the two transepts. The Prime Minister was accorded a seat by himself in The Theatre.

Admirals, generals, privy councillors and members of the Coronation Committee were seated in a gallery adjoining the south transept. Below them, in the south choir stall, were members of the diplomatic corps and ministers or their representatives from British countries overseas.

Above, in another gallery, were gathered the Masters and Scholars of Westminster School. As the monarch entered The Theatre they cried out in Latin (the only Latin used during the service), "Long Live King George VI." The Westminster Scholars have exercised this privilege of saluting the sovereign for the last twelve coronations.

Distinguished members of the public occupied the remaining galleries.

VI. The Coronation Service.

The Coronation Service was conducted by the Archbishop of Canterbury, assisted by the Dean of

Westminster, the Archbishop of York and the other Bishops.

1. *The Recognition.* The Archbishop of Canterbury presented the King to the assembly asking if they were willing to do homage and service to him. The assembly shouted, "God Save King George!" This was done four times as the Archbishop and King faced North, South, East and West.

2. *The Taking of the Oath.* This pledge to govern in accordance with established laws and customs was given by the King. He swore it on the Bible at the altar, and signed a copy of it. The King then returned to his Chair of State and the Archbishop of Canterbury read aloud the Declaration prescribed by Act of Parliament concerning the King's powers and government. This the King repeated aloud and also signed.

3. *The Communion.* The Communion Service was then commenced, being taken as far as the Oblation. Here it was interrupted for the anointing, as is the custom.

4. *The Anointing.* The King moved from his Chair of State to the Coronation Chair and was anointed by the Archbishop of Canterbury after having taken off his ermine cape, his robe and Cap of State. During the anointing, a pall of gold and silver brocade was held over his head by four knights of the Order of the Garter. At one time, the King was required to wear a cloth over his head until the

sacred oil had dried. Some authorities say that the pall derives from this ancient custom.

5. *The Robing.* The King was vested by the Dean of Westminster with the Colobium Sindonis, a white sleeveless surplice, and then the Supertunica, a coat of cloth of gold, around which was placed a sword belt.

6. *The Receiving of the Regalia.* The Lord Great Chamberlain touched the King's heels with the golden Spurs which were taken from the altar and then returned. The Archbishop gave the Jewelled Sword of State to the King, and it was girded on him by the Lord Great Chamberlain. This was returned to the altar also. The King was further robed with the Armill, a kind of stole, and the Royal Robe or Imperial Mantle of cloth of gold.

Seated again in the Coronation Chair, he received from the Archbishop the Orb, the Ring, which was placed on the fourth finger of his right hand, and the two sceptres.

7. *The Crowning.* The Archbishop, after consecrating St. Edward's Crown at the altar and praying, placed the crown on the King's head. Immediately the assembly cried, "God Save the King." The King was then presented with a Bible by the Archbishop as "the most valuable gift that the world affords."

8. *Inthronization.* His Majesty was lifted and seated in the King's throne, behind the Coronation Chair, by the Archbishops, Bishops and secular Offi-

cers of State. This act symbolizes the monarch taking possession of his throne and kingdom.

9. *Homage*. The King received homage first from the Archbishop of Canterbury and other clerics, next from the Princes of the Blood and the Royal Family and then from the Peers in the order of their degree, viz.: Dukes, Marquesses, Earls, Viscounts and Barons.

10. *Crowning of the Queen*. The crowning of Queen Elizabeth, consort of King George VI, followed in a shorter ceremony. For her Coronation, the Queen knelt upon the faldstool set before the altar. She did not use the Coronation Chair which is used only by the ruler. On the faldstool she was anointed, invested with her Regalia and crowned. She then went to her throne, first bowing to the King who sat upon his.

11. *Communion Continued*. The Communion service was then continued from the Offertory, their Majesties quitting their thrones and taking off their crowns to kneel before the altar. The King gave the bread and wine for the service to the Archbishop. The King's Oblation consisted of an altar cloth and an ingot of gold weighing one pound. The Queen's Oblation was an altar cloth and a mark weight (about eight ounces) of gold.

12. *The Blessing*. After returning to their Chairs of State and kneeling upon the faldstools before them, the King and Queen were blessed by the Archbishop.

VII. Their Majesties retired to King Edward's Chapel for a short rest. There the King was disrobed of his Royal Robe of State and arrayed in his robe of purple velvet. The King then put on the Imperial Crown.

VIII. The Procession as before conducted the King and Queen out of the Abbey, the King bearing the Sceptre with the Cross and the Orb, the Queen bearing in her right hand her Sceptre with the Cross and in her left, the Ivory Rod with the Dove. The King and Queen then re-entered the State Coach for a triumphal parade through the streets of London escorted by nobles, heralds and other officials.

BIBLIOGRAPHY

England—a history in four volumes by John Richard Green. Peter Fenelon Collier, New York.

5,000 Years of Gems and Jewelry by Frances Rogers and Alice Beard. Frederick A. Stokes Co., New York.

The Greater Abbeys of England by Abbot Gasquet. Dodd, Mead Co., New York.

A History of the Coronation by W. J. Passingham. Sampson, Low, London.

Jewels of Romance and Renown by Mary Abbott. T. Werner Laurie, Ltd., London.

The King's Crowning by Rev. R. H. Murray. John Murray, London.

The King's Guards by Henry Legge-Bourke. MacDonald and Co., Ltd., London.

The Life of William the Conqueror by Sarah Henry Benton. The Dial Press, New York.

Pageant and Ceremony of the Coronation by Charles Eyre Pascoe. D. Appleton and Co., New York.

Peter the Cruel by Edward Storer. John Lane Co.

Westminster Abbey by W. J. Loftie, B.A., F.S.A. Seeley Service and Co., Ltd., London.

Westminster Abbey Re-examined by W. R. Lethaby. Duckworth, London.

William the Conqueror by Frank Merry Stenton, M.A. G. P. Putnam's Sons, London and New York.

The Encyclopaedia Britannica.

The Coronation Supplements of the London *Times* and the London *Daily Telegraph,* published in May of 1937.

INDEX

NOTE: *The index has been compiled by name rather than by title. Thus Earls of Erroll will be found under Erroll, Earls of. Names beginning with a prefix will be found under the letter of the prefix as: de Montfort, listed under the letter "d."*

Minute details about the Coronation Ceremony of Britain are traced in this volume. **The traditions and their meanings are described.**